KU-251-797

MAX WEBER

A Skeleton Key

POLYTECHNIC LIBRARY
WOLVERHAMPTON
ACC. NO. 485... CLASS
CONTROL
DATE 23. FEB. 1990 WV WE...
WITHDRAWN

Randall Collins

Masters of Social Theory
Volume 3

Cover Photo: Culver Pictures

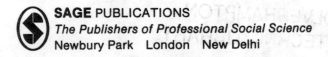

SAGE PUBLICATIONS
The Publishers of Professional Social Science
Newbury Park   London   New Delhi

Copyright © 1986 by Sage Publications, Inc.

All rights reserved. No part of this book may be reproduced or utilized in any form or by any means, electronic or mechanical, including photocopying, recording, or by any information storage and retrieval system, without permission in writing from the publisher.

For information address:

SAGE PUBLICATIONS, INC.
2111 W. Hillcrest Dr.
Newbury Park, CA 91320

SAGE PUBLICATIONS LTD
28 Banner Street
London EC1Y 8QE, England

SAGE PUBLICATIONS INDIA PVT LTD
M-32 Market, Greater Kailash I
New Delhi 110 048 India

Printed in the United States of America

Library of Congress Cataloging-in-Publication Data

Collins, Randall, 1941-
Max Weber: a skeleton key.

(Masters of social theory ; v. 3)
Includes index.
1. Weber, Max, 1864-1920. 2. Sociology—Germany—
History. I. Title. II. Series.
HM22.G3W4256 1985   301'.01   85-18340
ISBN 0-8039-2550-6
ISBN 0-8039-2551-4 (pbk.)

THIRD PRINTING, 1989

WOLVERHAMPTON
POLYTECHNIC LIBRARY

Contents

Series Editor's Introduction

This is the third volume in Sage's Masters of Social Theory series. Its subject, Max Weber, hardly needs an introduction. Nonetheless, let me offer a few opening observations on the merits of Randall Collins's approach to this master of social theory.

The subtitle, "A Skeleton Key," connotes several varied meanings, all of which capture the essence of the pages to follow. As the opening chapter documents, there is a Freudian skeleton in Max Weber's emotional closet. The inner conflicts that immobilized him for a number of years help explain the substance and profile of his most important sociological works. For without these conflicts, and the period of intellectual blockage that they produced, Weber might well have been easily forgotten in history as just another sociologist. There is, then, an important biographical element in Weber's sociology. The most straightforward meaning of "skeleton key" is the capacity to unlock doors; and in using Collins's key, this book becomes a way to gain access to the "hidden treasures" that lie buried in the volumes of historical detail in Weberian sociology. Collins does, I feel, a masterful job of opening doors for readers to catch a glimpse of not only the well-known portions of Weber's work but also the less well-publicized parts of his sociology, which, in many ways, are theoretically more important. Finally, this volume is a "skeleton outline" of Weberian sociology in its full comprehensiveness. In all of the chapters to follow, a concise description and scholarly analysis of Weber's most critical ideas are presented.

I must confess that contrary to most sociologists, I had never been overly fond of Weber's work. Its very strengths—rich and detailed empirical/historical description—had always overwhelmed and, all too frequently, rather bored me. Indeed, as Collins stresses, Weber was an empiricist at heart, but as Collins has amply demonstrated in his other theoretical projects, there is a great deal of positivist theorizing in Weber's detailed empirical descriptions. As a result, I have reappraised my earlier views on Weber; and even if one never shared my skepticism of Weber's work as theory, Collins makes a strong case for a positivistic interpretation of Weber's empirical descriptions. I have come to appreciate more fully that Weber's ideal-type methodology (when accompanied by his keen analytical sense and passion for historical detail) produces a vision of the basic organizing processes of human society as well as a series of generalizing statements, which, with little effort, can be translated into abstract sociological laws. Thus, one of the great strengths of this book is Collins's willingness to ignore Weber's own antipositivist statements and those of many contemporary "Weberians" for the purpose of demonstrating Weber's talent for sensing the basic and generic properties of human organization.

The other major contribution of this volume is the treatment of Weber's work as multidimensional and often contradictory. Weber's sociology is filled with unreconciled dimensions. The most important of these are the emphasis on ideas and the concern with material conditions. More than any other treatment of Weber that I have read, Collins's analysis highlights the multidimensionality of Weberian sociology and exposes Weber's own intellectual as well as personal conflicts over idealist versus materialist interpretations of historical processes. For as Collins clearly demonstrates, there are always political, economic, ecological, and conflictual forces operating simultaneously with religious, ideological, and cultural processes.

In closing, I trust that readers will appreciate how well Collins writes. The pages to follow are just fun to read. In all, this short book has made an important contribution to the corpus of secondary works on Max Weber.

Laguna Beach, California   —*Jonathan H. Turner*

1

Weber's Life and Personality

Melodramatics and Psychological Mysteries

For many sociologists, Max Weber is the great master. He was intellectually the most comprehensive and historically the most learned of any of the leaders of the discipline. He asked the most profound questions, and disciplined himself against accepting easy answers. What is the nature of modern society? What is the pattern of world history? And, personally and politically, how can one act responsibly and morally in a world in which the hard realities of economics, power, and organization always assert themselves? Weber probed the depths of these questions; the concepts and theories that he turned up on the way have become a major part of sociology's intellectual equipment.

At the same time, Weber is nothing if not controversial. For some he was a hero who went out of his way to defend the underdog and entered numerous disputes and lawsuits on their behalf; a man of honor who took moral responsibility in such a punctilious way that he would never accept an advantage for himself or deprive others of what he felt was their due. For others, though, Weber was very far from a saint. He is described as a conservative, even militaristic, nationalist, whose doctrines of authority have paved the way for the Nazi dictatorship.

Intellectually, too, Weber has provoked endless debates. Did he succeed in turning the tables on the Marxists, making religion more powerful than economics instead of an ideological reflection of it? Or was he a more sophisticated developer of Marxian themes into multiple dimensions of conflict? Was he a precursor of Parsonian functionalism, or its most powerful antidote? Was he an action theorist, upholding the meaningful cognitions of the individual over the impersonal laws of a scientific system? Was he an evolutionist, as modern German commentators have interpreted his views of world history, or an anti-evolutionist who defended the multiple paths and unpredictable shifts of a historicist vision?

The truth is, Weber seems to have been all these things and more. Especially on the intellectual side, Weber offers something for almost every interpretation. This no doubt is one of the reasons he has been so influential. Parsonian functionalists, anti-Marxists, idealists, and evolutionists can all find materials to build upon in Weber. So can antifunctionalists who wish to assimilate Weber to the subjectivism of symbolic interactionism or social phenomenology. At the same time, Weber provided tools for radical critics such as C. Wright Mills, and deserves his reputation as a progenitor of modern conflict theory. At times, Weber is the defender of the influence of ideas upon history; at other times, he offers compelling analyses of the church as a purely material institution.

One way to resolve these apparent contradictions is to say that the essence of Weber was to be multidimensional. One of his most important formulations, used in the theories both of stratification and of politics, is the tripartite distinction among *class, status,* and *power:* or if you like, among economics, ideas and beliefs, and politics. All three realms exist; all three have independent effects; and each influences the others. Weber's lifelong works, whether dealing with the origins and nature of capitalism, the problems of religion, or the issues of politics, all involve the applications of this multidimensional mode of analysis to every question.

And yet, we may legitimately ask whether or not Weber himself really felt it was this way: whether or not the world is simply so many interacting dimensions, with no final resting point, and nothing counting more heavily than anything else. For there are many instances in his writings in which Weber seems to be predominantly an idealist, bent on defending the role of ideas, of the human mind, of ideal factors such as religion and rationality as the master-determinants of world history. Some scholars have interpreted him in this way, and, personally, I am not inclined to disagree that this may well have been where Weber's heart really was. On the other hand, as a practicing sociologist, I would have to say that the aspects of Weber's intellectual influence that have proved most fruitful are those that stress exactly the opposite viewpoint: that is, Weber as a conflict theorist, Weber as a man who best understood raw power politics, military struggle, and the difficult material constraints of groups and formal organization. And this side of Weber's writings is equally real, constituting hundreds of pages of sheer sociological realism, even cynicism.

In his recent search for a truly multidimensional theory for sociology, Jeffrey Alexander (1983) describes Weber's work as a failure of multidimensionality. By this he means that Weber deals with multiple dimensions of society, and even discusses explicitly the multidimensional nature of the world; yet the final product seems to be merely inconsistent, rather than a true synthesis. I agree with this conclusion. Weber's writings are somewhat schizophrenic. It is not that he directly contradicts himself, or fails to handle each question thoroughly; but in his voluminous works, one can find almost anything one looks for. There is plenty of material for Parsons's functionalism, with its emphasis upon values, and also for Schluchter or Habermas's rationalist evolutionism. Weber is a legitimate ally of the symbolic interactionists, as well as an influence upon Alfred Schutz, who in turn influenced social phenomenology and ethnomethodology. On the other hand, modern organization theory and stratification theory could reasonably emerge from Weber's work, and he could influence conflict sociologists such as C. Wright Mills, or me, for all these elements are present in Weber. They don't add up to one grand synthesis; it would be more accurate to say there are several different Webers, all coexisting within the same body of work.

Because of this "schizophrenic" quality in Weber's work, I think it is worthwhile to spend a certain amount of attention on his life and personality. This is certainly not a full-scale intellectual biography showing where his various ideas came from and how they developed over his lifetime. Nothing like that kind of biographical study has yet been accomplished and this brief introduction would hardly be the place to attempt it. Weber's wife wrote a long set of biographical reminiscences (Marianne Weber, 1926/1975), but this does not analyze his intellectual development in any depth, and offers a somewhat idealized, even censored, view of him as a person. What is interesting about Weber's life is the fact that it contains the same quality we find in his intellectual work, that of being torn between extremes. Weber had a somewhat tortured career, punctuated by a long period of mental breakdown in the middle. Though he began with high political and academic prospects, his career was interrupted just as it seemed to get going. Only relatively late in his life did he make a comeback into the realm of political power and intellectual eminence that he seemed to have had waiting for him at the outset. It is worthwhile to look into the nature of his breakdown, I think, because it casts light on just the things that created intellectual tension in his work.

WEBER'S CAREER PATTERN

The main facts of Weber's life are soon told. He was born on April 21, 1864, the eldest son of a German lawyer and politician, himself from a family of linen manufacturers. The family lived in Berlin, where the elder Weber was an important member of the German Reichstag, representing a middle-of-the-road party of industrialists' interests. Young Max met numerous important politicians and intellectuals at his father's house, and very early acquired a sophisticated insider's view of the world. He studied law at the Universities of Heidelberg and Berlin, belonged to a dueling fraternity, and did his military service and became a reserve officer in the army. His law degree ushered him into a career in the courts, and at the same time he continued advanced studies in the history of law and economics, which opened his prospects for academic positions as well. (Such combinations of legal, political, and academic positions were not uncommon among the higher administrative classes in Germany at this time.) Weber became active in a number of political associations, especially the *Verein für Sozialpolitik*, which was an association of academic economists interested in social reform. He became known for his research on the problem of foreign farm-workers displacing German farmers along the eastern (Polish) border of Germany.

In 1893, Weber married Marianne Schnitger, a cousin who was later to become one of the leaders of the German feminist movement. The next year he became a professor of economics at the University of Freiburg, in southern Germany. In 1896, he became a professor of political science at the University of Heidelberg. A year later, his father died after a stormy argument with his son. Within months, Max fell ill from a condition of nervous exhaustion that made it impossible for him to speak in public or go to work. After a series of leaves of absence from his professorship, and unsuccessful stays in several sanatoriums, he finally resigned from his university position, as well as from political activity.

Finally, in 1903, after almost six years of crippling illness, he began to work again, although the nervous ailment troubled him throughout most of the rest of his life. He produced *The Protestant Ethic and the Spirit of Capitalism* and various methodological essays, and took over the editorship of a journal in which he published most of his works. He became active in founding the German Sociological Society and in organizing its research projects. He traveled widely, engaged in numerous lawsuits and public controversies, and began to edit an encyclopedic handbook of social economics, for which he himself wrote a massive volume, *Economy and Society*. His house at Heidelberg became a center for important German intellectuals, and he became friends with some of Freud's radical followers.

With the outbreak of World War I in 1914, Weber's military commission was activated and he became an administrator of military hospitals. As the German war effort faltered, Weber became politically active in the movement to bring about a negotiated peace. To fill his journal, he published the results of his research on the religions of China, India, and ancient Judaism. In the political turmoil as the Kaiser's government fell at the end of the war, Weber began to gain political prominence. He was temporarily elected to the revolutionary workers' and soldiers' council in Heidelberg; was part of the German delegation to the Versailles peace conference that negotiated the war settlement; and was active in the founding of a centrist, German democratic party. For the first time in over twenty years, he began teaching again, at the universities of Vienna and Munich. Attempting to steer a middle ground between left-wing revolutionaries and right-wing nationalists, he delivered powerful speeches on such topics as "Scholarship as a Vocation" and "Politics as a Vocation," and lectured both on general economic history and on socialism. He also brought out his collected writings. In the midst of all this activity, he suddenly contracted pneumonia and died on June 14, 1920, at the age of 56.

Notice that Weber's life pattern seems to revolve around his breakdown. Before it, his intellectual work was relatively un-distinguished, at least compared to the work on sociology for which he

later became famous. He did produce several lengthy works, but they
were rather conventional, specialized academic scholarship on questions
of legal and economic history, and a policy study of farm workers living
on the Polish border—something like a study of Mexican farm workers
in the U.S. Southwest would be today. To the extent that Weber did
write about sociological concepts more generally, he seemed to have
formed many of the ideas that he expressed later; but this was not at all
what he considered worth writing about. On the other hand, after his
breakdown, he published *The Protestant Ethic* as virtually the first work
of his new phase of intellectual life. Before his breakdown, he worked on
rather mundane political and economic issues; afterward, he shifted his
attention toward religion and the role of ideas, as expressed in his essays
about ideal types, *verstehen,* and questions of values in politics and in
scholarship. The earlier Weber does not disappear, but another side of
him comes into the open as well. It seems likely that had the breakdown
not occurred, the famous Weberian sociology that we know would not
have come into existence.

WEBER'S BREAKDOWN AND ITS CAUSES

What then was Weber's breakdown? Today we would certainly
regard it as a neurosis, psychological in its origins. Weber was a
contemporary of Freud, but none of the doctors he saw in 1898 had any
inkling of psychotherapy; they prescribed rest, travel, and stays in a
mountain sanatorium, where the regimen consisted of baths, diets, and
physical exercise. None of this did any good, and Weber became a
semi-invalid for a number of years, withdrawing from all active work
until later, when his condition gradually began to improve.

Weber's health had always been excellent. He had been a hard
worker, an active social and political participant, known for his rousing
speeches to classrooms or meetings, and for drinking beer and talking
endlessly with admiring colleagues and followers. The trouble started in
a long-standing battle between his mother and father. They differed
both in political and in moral attitudes, as well as about how she was to
run the household. The father, a self-important man of the traditional
patriarchal type, expected automatic deference from his wife and
children alike, as well as her devotion to his demands. After several of
their children had married and moved away from home, the mother,

Helene Weber, had disputes with her husband over how long she would stay and at what times she might go to visit them. The father, Max Sr., wanted the visits scheduled according to his convenience. In the summer of 1897, such a dispute broke out over Helene's planned visit to Max Jr. and Marianne at Heidelberg. The father eventually came along and tried to lay down the law in the presence of his son. With his usual sense of righteous honor in defending the underdog, Max angrily took his mother's part, and laid down an ultimatum to his father: He would break all ties with him unless he agreed to a pact that guaranteed his mother certain rights to make visits without his father's permission. Max Sr. angrily refused, and the son threw him out of the house (figuratively speaking, of course). Before anyone did anything to reconcile, the father huffily went off on a trip with a friend. Only his body came back: He was dead of a gastric hemorrhage.

Helene Weber, it seemed, soon adjusted herself to whatever grief this caused her. Max, too, at first seemed little disturbed. But in the winter, he began to feel continually exhausted. He felt feverish and tense. Formerly a sound sleeper, he now became an insomniac. Even sleeping drugs provided little relief, and his days left him harried and unable to focus on his work. Lecturing became a torment for him, and he could no longer bring himself to face an audience. By the winter of 1898, his illness had worsened and included physical symptoms, and his arms and back became paralyzed when he tried to trim the Christmas tree. Only travel brought him any distraction. He spent much time in Switzerland and Italy, looking at the sights, or lying on a couch, trying to think of nothing. Finally, after several years of this, he improved enough so he could begin to read books, "anything but literature in my own field." After four years of almost complete enervation, he slowly began to work again at writing, and eventually recovered his ability to attend meetings and make speeches. But for years the thought of delivering university lectures was a terror for him, and, in general, any pressure to write something by compulsion or under a deadline would bring a relapse into the sleeplessness and tension of his breakdown.

What could have been going on? By a modern interpretation, the tension and exhaustion were due to a strong inner conflict. All his energy was being used up by two opposing forces, which canceled each other out and kept him more or less paralyzed. There was obviously, too, a strong repression, certain thoughts that Weber did not want to think about, but that nevertheless obsessively demanded his attention and would not let him think of anything else. The inability to sleep, as

Freud would have pointed out, protected him from these thoughts
breaking through in the form of dreams, and lying on a couch during the
daytime trying to keep his mind blank did the same thing for him while
he was awake.

Now what was he trying to repress? The obvious answer would be the
guilt he felt at having caused his father's death. But this explanation does
not seem sufficient, because Weber was the kind of person who believed
in freely admitting any moral guilt. Moreover, his mother, who was an
even more moralistic person, and who was just as involved in the dispute
as he was, set an example of getting over the crisis soon enough. The
contradictory, mutually neutralizing forces that had him in their grasp
require further analysis.

Mother's Versus Father's Moral and Political Ideals. Weber's mother
and father held strongly different moral and political positions, and the
conflict between the two of them became strongly engrained in Max's
personality. His father was a highly placed politician. Though not
personally very charismatic, he was involved in the central goings-on at
the Reichstag as well as in running the Berlin municipal government.
Prominent politicians as well as elite academic intellectuals gathered at
his house, and young Max grew up in an atmosphere where he heard
both principled conversations and the daily political gossip and plans of
the capitol decision makers. Max clearly enough identified with his
father's career and in general shared his political sympathies. His father
was a National Liberal, belonging to a bourgeois party that supported
Chancellor Bismarck in his struggle against both the Socialists, and
against the political privileges of the Catholic church. In general, from
his father Weber learned of the practical realities of politics and the need
for compromise. Max Sr. himself was rather easygoing and self-satis-
fied, and not at all moralistic.

The mother was of a very different temper. Raised in a pious, but
theologically liberal Christian family, she believed strongly that the
church must make its way in the modern world by divesting itself of
traditional dogmas and ceremonies and devoting itself to ameliorating
the lot of the poor. Only thus could they be saved from godless
socialism. Personally, she moralized over every detail of daily life. While
her husband controlled the household finances in the old patriarchal
way, she plotted and scrimped to find money to give to charities and to
her favorite political causes. While her husband distinctly held to
middle-of-the-road, establishment-oriented politics, she favored the
new Christian-social, welfare-oriented movements that were springing
up in the liberal wing of the churches.

Young Max, although he had absorbed his political education from his father, was nevertheless drawn into these movements by his mother's pressure. In 1890, he and his mother together attended the founding of the Evangelical-Social Congress, a new party that favored both the monarchy and social welfare. It sought to use the traditional powers of the Emperor to bypass the selfish interests of capitalists and revolutionaries, and save the workers from Marxism by bringing down social welfare from above. Max became a member of the association and a close friend of one of its leaders. This was the so-called poor people's pastor, Friedrich Naumann, a charismatic and idealistic preacher. Weber became Naumann's adviser on the practical realities of economics and politics. Weber succeeded in influencing him to add a nationalist twist to their program: for, as Max argued, it was essential for Germany to remain a great power in the world if it was to have the means to create a decent life for the masses. Where would social welfare be, he warned, if the Cossacks came?—echoing a long-standing German fear of the need for defense against the barbaric autocracy that they saw threatening them from Russia.

Here, then, was one possible conflict occurring within Max Weber. His mother's pious moralism had a powerful effect on him. Although his father had smoothed his way into the political world, his mother had captured his political allegiance. Throughout his life, his political convictions were to lie especially on the side of the religious welfare-oriented liberals. It is true, though, that Weber was more realistic than they, and saw the tremendous obstacles to their practical success. He also introduced a tone of conservative nationalism into their policies, which made the power-prestige of the state paramount because he felt it was prerequisite to everything else. Later, when he criticized the German government's policy prior to World War I and its conduct during the war itself, it was from the ultrarealistic viewpoint that the Kaiser and his chosen politicians were bungling things badly, isolating Germany from all allies and needlessly bringing in the United States on the side of its enemies. Weber regarded the pacifists among his friends as unrealistic dreamers, who intruded moral viewpoints into politics but did not offer any means of defending themselves. In a sense, then, Weber compromised between the idealism of his mother and the practical realism of his father: though he wished to defend his mother's ideals, he agreed with his father that, in politics, to insist on being idealistic all the time was merely a way of courting defeat. As he said to a group of young socialist idealists at the end of World War I, who felt that propertyless utopian communes would be the way to rebuild society: "Faith can move mountains but not remedy ruined finances and lack of capital" (Marianne Weber, 1926/1975: 631).

One of Weber's inner conflicts, then, probably revolved around the differences between his father and mother. Most obviously these differences were manifested as political, which kept him immobilized in pursuing his own political career. But even more, they were manifested as conflicting personality styles. Though outwardly Max Weber resembled his father, inwardly his mother ruled. On the outside, one could see the rather corpulent, stern young patriarch, giving orders to his students and then treating them to a beer-drinking contest; the young man proud of his military uniform and his fraternity dueling scars, defending the necessity of capitalism and of a powerful German state. On the inside, though, his mother's incessant moralizing had taken firm possession, and he was never able to do anything without endless wrangling over taking the purest and most righteous possible stance, a sort of compulsive nobility to all concerned. The two sides of his personality seemed to be locked in a paralyzing symbiosis.

Sexual Repression. A more straightforward Freudian explanation could also be given. Freud's classical theory of the Oedipus complex concerns the unconscious desires, which he believed existed in every male child, to possess his mother sexually and kill his father, his main sexual rival. In a sense, Max Weber did kill his father, and one could ascribe his neurosis to guilt resulting from this. In traditional Freudian theory, it is the son's identification with his father, his internalization as the superego, that produces the guilt, as well as sexual inhibitions. In Max's case, however, it appears that his mother was by far the more puritanical, moralistic figure, and it is her moral attitudes that he had internalized.

Helene Weber, as we have seen, was a very religious person, full of active social conscience. She was also an extreme puritan in matters of sex. She regarded even marital intercourse as a sin, a sacrifice undergone only for the sake of procreation. When she was younger, she longed for old age to free her of this obligation (Marianne Weber, 1926/1975: 30). It seems clear, then, that one of the sources of conflict with her pleasure-loving, unmoralistic husband was over sex. Unable to control her husband, Helene Weber made up for it by redoubling her efforts to control her sons: in the case of Max, apparently quite successfully. In his university days and during military service, when his compatriots were cheerfully whoring around, Max seems to have remained unyielding and pure. At least, this is what his wife reports in her heavily euphemistic biography: "Without using words—for in those days the dark substrata of life and their menacing problems were left under thick wraps—and only through the holy purity of her being, she [Helene Weber] had implanted in him indestructible inhibitions against a surrender to his drives" (Marianne Weber, 1926/1975: 91).

Now Marianne herself, whom Max married in 1893 (when he was 29 and she 23), was like his mother in many respects. She too was sexually quite puritanical and worried about whether or not she would be able to stand the "heavy sacrifice" of conjugal marital duties (Marianne Weber, 1926/1975: 189). Apparently she was not able to make the sacrifice; not only did she never have children, but their marriage was sexually unconsummated (Green, 1974; Mitzman, 1970). But unlike Max's own parents, there seems not to have been any conflict about this; Marianne had picked a husband who was as fully inhibited as herself. Perhaps, one might say, his mother helped pick her out for him. For Marianne was a distant cousin from a poorer branch of the Weber family who had come to stay with the Webers in Berlin. Sharing the same kind of religious and moral attitudes, she became a close friend of Max's mother well before her relationship with him developed. Their courtship was hardly an erotic one. Marianne describes him as treating her as might a benevolent uncle (Marianne Weber, 1926/1975: 175). There was some moral questioning, so characteristic of both of them, about his duties to an invalid cousin to whom Max had formed some vague attachment five years earlier. Finally, he proposed marriage to Marianne, by mail, in a "love letter" that is surprisingly pompous, overbearing, and even preachy. It talks about their decision as a "struggle of souls," makes a demand for "clarity" and "sobriety," and contains such statements as "We must not tolerate any fanciful surrender to unclear and mystical moods in our souls" (Marianne Weber, 1926/1975: 179). It is not without justification that Max says to her in another letter, "What an old bachelor you have taken for yourself, my child" (Marianne Weber, 1926/1975: 181).

They married when Max acquired a professorship at Freiburg, which enabled him to move from his parents' home in Berlin—he had been living at home all this time, which was typical in that era—and set up his own household. He plunged into a great amount of academic and political work. Marianne reports that he worked until 1:00 a.m. every

night, then immediately fell asleep: which indicates both how they
avoided sex, and the fact that, unlike later, he had no difficulty sleeping.

The argument with his father, and the ensuing breakdown, occurred
after four years of this routine. Marianne reports that they were very
happy, except for Max's overload of work, though she was hardly the
person to uncover, or admit, any signs of sexual tension. (In her 700-
page biography, she never admits a single instance of conflict or even
disagreement between them; she describes it as a perfectly idyllic
relationship.) But it is a reasonable hypothesis that sexual tension could
have been an underlying force in the breakdown. Max had always taken
his mother's side in her long-standing guerilla war against her husband.
And although of course such a thing would never, *never* be mentioned,
he could have sensed the underlying battle over sexual repression that
went on between them. His father represented sexual freedom (quite
possibly he had a mistress or visited prostitutes on the side, a well-
known phenomenon in the Victorian era, when many women shared
Helene Weber's puritanism), but his mother was vehemently moralistic,
above all on the question of sex. Thus when Max helped bring about his
father's death through the shock of breaking off their family ties, it
might well have begun to dawn on him that in siding with his mother on
all her moralistic demands, he had cut off something healthy that his
father represented: ordinary human sexual drives. Not only that, but
Max could easily have begun to feel an unconscious rebellion and even a
hatred of his puritanical mother, who helped kill his father and felt not
even a pang of guilt about it. Perhaps *this* was the realization that he
could not bear to think about, that kept him sleepless at night, and
striving to think of nothing during his days.

Other circumstantial evidence supports this interpretation. For we do
know, thanks to revelations made decades later by the women involved,
that Max actually did begin to have illicit affairs. The main figure was
Else von Richthofen, a woman who was a member of avant-garde circles
and believed in sexual liberation, and whose sister Frieda married the
British erotic novelist, D. H. Lawrence (in 1912). Their affair lasted a
number of years, beginning about 1907, it appears, when Weber himself
became acquainted with the rebellious younger intellectuals. These were
precisely the years during which Max recovered his energies and began
to formulate ambitious projects and engage in public controversies: as if
the rediscovery of his sexuality brought him back to life again. But it
may also be significant that Max first met Else von Richthoven in 1897,
the same year of the fight with his father and the beginning of his
breakdown.

Else was a student in Max's university classes. From today's perspective that sounds routine enough, but at the time a female studying at a university was a major event. Feminists had just begun to demand for German women the right to attend universities and pursue careers; prior to this time, only poorer women worked, and the goal of any female of the respectable classes was to become married and to preside over her house. Weber's attitude toward women was at first chivalrous but condescending (as we can see in the above quotations from his letters), but as his own wife became a strong feminist, he followed her and became a resolute advocate of feminism. Thus he used his university position to allow Marianne to break the barrier against women students, and she and Else von Richthoven attended his classes together (Marianne Weber, 1926/1975: 229). The ironic part may well be that this is what first aroused Max's erotic interest in women. For Else, though a feminist friend of his wife, was far more adventuresome and did not share her friend's puritanical inclinations. Thus the time when the showdown with Max's father occurred could very well have been when Max's erotic life was awakening. Whether or not anything came of it at that time (I am inclined to believe that it didn't), this was the very woman he would have an affair with later. Of course his own moralistic tendencies were also at their height, as evidenced by his outburst on behalf of his mother; thus setting up the paralyzing conflict between opposing forces that became the essence of his illness.

It is in keeping with this interpretation that Weber's illness diminished in the latter part of his life. When the omnipresent pressure of his wife and mother began to recede, he began to make long trips on his own. (Presumably this provided the opportunity for his sexual affairs.) Marianne Weber was becoming a successful feminist leader, publishing her own books and involved in organizing and speech making. Later, when women's suffrage was acquired at the end of World War I, she became the first woman to be elected to public office in Germany, as elected representative in the state legislature of Baden (southern Germany). Marianne's growing independence thus may have helped Max's psychological independence. Else von Richthofen, too, was not far away. In 1902, she married Edgar Jaffe, a friend of Weber's who was also his business partner in launching the journal he edited, the *Archiv für Sozialwissenschaft (Archive for Social Science)*. One might suppose that, given Max's intricately developed sense of moral responsibility, an adulterous relationship with the wife of a friend would have put a lot of strain upon him; but in fact, the outcome seems to have been just the opposite. This too fits the interpretation that Weber's neurosis was a struggle for awakening sexual freedom, after an enforced pattern of extreme repression upheld by his mother and wife.

It is ironic that some of these themes actually came through on the surface of Max and Marianne's life, although neither she (nor presumably he) ever consciously recognized what was going on. In the years from around 1906 onward, when Max began to take part again in an active social and intellectual life, their circle became increasingly concerned, even obsessed, with the question of sexual liberation. This was partly a matter of Freud's influence. The publication of *The Interpretation of Dreams* in 1900 had made Freud famous, and the early years of the twentieth century were a time when his first major theoretical work on sex came out. The Victorian era was breaking down, and Germany and England were the main places in which the sexual liberation was happening. (The American writer F. Scott Fitzgerald became famous a few years later for describing the same breakdown in the United States at about the time of World War I.) The feminist movement, too, was tied into this liberalization. Although many of the older feminists, such as Marianne Weber, were extreme puritans, the very unconventionality of the movement, and the entrance of women into public careers, meant that the old ideas of respectability were undergoing some rethinking. Thus Marianne's feminist friends, as well as Max's intellectual connections, brought the question of erotic liberation into discussions in their own home.

As Marianne describes it, she and Max saw eye to eye on these issues. Although they were willing to listen and take part in debates with their younger friends, their own attitude was to defend the sanctity of the traditional marriage and traditional restrictive attitudes toward sex. Given their own absence of sex in marriage, this was somewhat ironic, and perhaps some awareness of the extreme nature of their own practice was responsible for a softening of their attitudes, to the extent that they were willing to be forgiving of other persons, "less strong than themselves," who had sexual lapses (Marianne Weber, 1926/1975: 371-389). Of what Max himself felt, we cannot be sure. When a radical young Freudian, Dr. Otto Gross, submitted an article to Weber's journal, Weber refused to publish it and wrote a vehement denunciation of its doctrine. Supposing one did succeed in bringing back, through Freud's methods, some long-repressed memory of sexual "misconduct," Weber argued; how would this help the individual if he or she did not take *ethical* responsibility for it (Marianne Weber, 1926/1975: 379)? In other words, Weber completely missed Freud's central point: that it was exactly this ethical responsibility, the guilt-producing pressure of the superego, that caused the repression and neurosis in the first place.

But even if Weber had no intellectual or personal understanding of the dynamics of the repression that had so obviously afflicted him, he worked out a practical *modus vivendi* with his erotic life. Marianne herself noticed that their attitudes became more sympathetic to the newer ideals of "norm-free eroticism"; not only was it a favorite conversational topic, but they came to agree that though monogamy was best, it could not be forced on everyone. Max spent much time on vacation amid the radical intellectual colony that lived in the Italian Alps. In Marianne's eyes, he was merely acting as a protector to them, straightening out their legal affairs with the police. For example, he helped the wife of Otto Gross, the same man whose Freudian article he had rejected, to get custody of her children when the state wished to take them from her because she had been living with an anarchist (Marianne Weber, 1926/1975: 486-487). Max was to maintain his radical connections in politics too, despite his conservatism. When Germany broke down into revolution at the end of World War I, he helped get his young revolutionary pacifist friends out of jail and testified on their behalf at numerous trials. Marianne put all this down to his innate chivalry, though it would be more plausible to say that he thrived on the sexual liberation of these circles.

Marianne was touched by Max's refusal to take a superior moral attitude toward those who were "sinning"; she believed that when he referred to his own sins he meant an old guilt over leaving an invalid sweetheart to marry Marianne, or the guilt over the death of his father (Marianne Weber, 1926/1975: 389). But whatever the blindness or the rationalizations, they worked out a way of life that enabled Max to recover something like normalcy. And there were intellectual consequences too, for when he came to write on the sociology of the family, his position was as far removed as imaginable from the sentimental Victorian ideology in which he was brought up. His sociology of the family is a realistic analysis of conflict, of the weapons of male dominance and war between the sexes, in which marriage is a harsh relationship of sex and economics, only occasionally glossed over by sentiment.

Political Versus Intellectual Careers. There is a third factor that must have been implicated in Weber's breakdown. His early life was a struggle between alternative careers: political or academic. The result of his breakdown was that he withdrew from both of them, and ended up doing intellectual work of a sort he had previously regarded as merely a frivolous pastime.

In his early adult life, Weber entirely expected to have an active career in public affairs. Not only did he follow the footsteps of his father in his legal training, but his energies were mainly devoted to lengthy reports on issues of political reform (the migrant labor problem, the stock market), which he wrote for activist political associations. The Evangelical-Social group to which he belonged regarded him as a future politician, and Max himself considered the academic work he produced at the university in legal and economic scholarship as merely a way of filling his leisure hours while waiting for the proper political position to open up (Marianne Weber, 1926/1975: 162-164). But that was exactly the problem. The Christian-welfare group with which he was active had little prospects amidst the tides of German party politics at the time, and Max was realistic enough to know it very well. His own mother was blithely oblivious to political realities. After her husband's death, she used the family money to finance the political campaigns of Naumann ("the poor people's pastor"), though he failed initially for several tries to win a Reichstag seat (Marianne Weber, 1926/1975: 223). His father's more conservative, National Liberal party, too, was losing ground, as German politics divided more sharply between the Marxian socialists and right-wing parties.

Thus Weber more or less drifted into an academic career, not because he wished it, but because positions became available to him while politics was getting him nowhere. He may have felt, too, the pressure between his mother, who swept him along into supporting her moralistic favorites, and his father, the cooler political head whose attitudes Max always regarded as more rational, if less inspired. And it was in the spring of 1897, before the breakdown, that Max had been offered a chance to run for a Parliamentary seat (but as a Liberal, his father's party) (Marianne Weber, 1926/1975: 224). Max turned it down. The political road seemed blocked: both, it seems, by objective conditions, and by his mother's pressures, which kept him tied to unrealistically utopian positions.

The fact is, Weber probably would not have been a very good politician. Although he understood politics extremely well and in his political writings always recognized that sheer unbending moralism was largely a formula for disaster, nevertheless in his personal behavior he always took the most extreme moralistic stances. Thus after he returned to public activity about 1908, he became involved in a number of controversies in the newspapers and the law courts. In every case, he started out with a good cause, which then degenerated into a string of accusations and recriminations (Marianne Weber, 1926/1975: 408-449). When a newspaper wrote insultingly about his wife's feminist movement, Max helped her draft a reply, then became involved in a slander suit that eventually hinged on the identity of an anonymous professor who was allegedly being quoted. Characteristically, just when Weber was winning the slander trial, he switched his sympathies, because he did not wish the professor on the other side, who had been caught committing a deception, to be crushed by the verdict. In another case, Weber found himself in a lawsuit because of the intemperate way he criticized a university official for questioning the motives of a pacifist; and Weber was opposed to pacifism himself! An unseemly legal wrangle even broke out over the publication of a new edition of a handbook of political economy, which Weber was to edit. Another professor, who had apparently been passed over for the editorship, sued on the grounds that the new edition would deprive the aged heirs of the editor of the old edition, now long since deceased, of their continued royalties. The case was absurd, but Weber ultimately challenged the man to a duel with sabers (it did not come off). No wonder Weber's contemporaries regarded him as something of a medieval knight, stuck by mistake in the modern world.

In short, although Weber knew better intellectually, in practice he took politics in just the fanatically moralistic way his mother advocated. No doubt he was better off in the academic world. But this was not what he wanted. Although he was a charismatic lecturer, he always felt lecturing was a burden. Some of the same conflicts showed up there. He held firmly to the doctrine of value-freedom, that academic work ought to be above politics, and that the professor ought to refrain from trying to indoctrinate his students. Nevertheless, he did not live up to his own injunction very well. His inaugural speech at Freiburg, his first university position, was a strongly nationalist statement of political priorities. Years later, when he returned to teaching at the University of Munich at the end of World War I, he interrupted his scholarly lectures a number of times to give his own stern commentaries on the current political situation. His moral belief that a professor ought to be value free, and his equally strong tendency to moralize about what he considered to be politically right, always created tension for him. In the years after his breakdown in 1897, the tension literally kept him from speaking at all.

His neurosis gave him the excuse to drop both politics and academics. In fact, if Freud's doctrine is correct that a neurosis solves a practical problem by removing the patient from some situation he or she does not wish to deal with, it is clear that Weber's breakdown was an ideal way to avoid both sides of his career conflict. The one thing he could not stand, even in his years of recovery, was deadlines or work under compulsion. When he began to read again after years of mental blankness, it was "anything but works in my own field." What he did read was ancient history, oriental and medieval religion, and later, art, philosophy, and history of music and culture. This is of course what he has become famous for analyzing in his sociology. But Weber himself never seemed to have regarded it as very serious work. Although we might consider this pure academics, for Weber his academic specialty was the mundane, practical analysis of problems of economics and law. Later, when he had recovered enough to become active in the German Sociological Association, the researches he proposed, and to some extent carried out, were far from the historical areas that have made him famous. Instead, he felt that practical knowledge should be gained regarding the effects of factory work on the life of workers, the effects of the popular press, and of social clubs on the political consciousness of the masses—all good, topical, reform-oriented issues. Weber's dominant "healthy" state of mind seems to have taken seriously only the kind of practical social issues in which his mother had been interested.

Fortunately for sociology, Weber's breakdown put him in the position in which he had nothing to do but indulge his more "frivolous" intellectual interests, especially on religion and on exotic, faraway societies. His sense of obligation helped in this regard too. After he agreed to join his friends in editing the *Archiv* in 1903, he felt he should keep it supplied with materials. It was for this journal that he wrote his *Protestant Ethic* and his methodological essays, as well as his other studies of the world religions. Then the publisher of the journal, who was also a personal friend, got him to agree to edit the encyclopedia of political science. When various contributers failed to meet their obligations, Weber felt he had to fill in the missing spaces. Hence his contribution grew into the voluminous treatise on sociology, his *Economy and Society*. For Weber, this was merely a duty, a sideshow of his main interests, although for subsequent sociology, it is his masterwork. His famous studies of Indian ˚religion, too, and of ancient Judaism, were reports he worked on during World War I, as a respite from his futile political efforts to bring a negotiated peace (Marianne Weber, 1926/1975: 570, 593). (If the book on Judaism gives a much more political interpretation of religion than his other books, it is partly due to the fact that he was working on it in the midst of such a political atmosphere.)

Intellectually, then, Weber emerges as a many-sided figure. One aspect of his personality felt it was proper only to work on rather mundane economic issues of immediate application. Another side of him loved to work on the farthest reaches of historical and religious comparison. Although this was where his real genius lay, he never could do it except when accidents of his life made it possible (or when he had to fill a request to produce historical lectures or a historical handbook). And in the years when he was recovering from his neurosis, living and having affairs among the young bohemian intellectuals, he occasionally indulged an artistic side of his personality. Around 1911, he became very interested in modern art, in musical performances, and planned to write a sociology embracing all the arts (Marianne Weber, 1926/1975: 496-500). He also planned a book on Tolstoy, the Russian novelist. Weber declared that the book would contain the results of his innermost experiences (Marianne Weber, 1926/1975: 466). Presumably this meant that he would deal with the moral issue of pacifism, of which Tolstoy was a famous leader, and which, along with sex, agitated Weber's intellectual friends. And because one of Tolstoy's most famous books was a novel of adultery, *Anna Karenina,* we might have been treated to Weber's own revelations about sexual morality. But this dream of Weber's never materialized. All that appeared of this artistic interest was his short volume on the sociology of music. But even his artistic concerns added something to his overall sociological vision. As we shall see, one of his major themes may be summed up as a concern for the cultural significance of world history, and especially of the modern world.

WEBER'S MULTISIDED INTELLECTUAL PERSONALITY

It may be that we have not cracked the secret of Weber's personality. But I hope to have made the case for seeing his neurotic breakdown as a key, or at least an emblem, of the multisidedness that is his strongest intellectual characteristic. A neurosis, particularly of the paralyzing sort he experienced, is a conflict between strong opposing forces. We have seen that Weber was subject to numerous such conflicts. And though they were personally debilitating, they were not trivial ones but reflections of some of the major forces of his world. His father and mother, with their opposing political and moral attitudes, were representatives of several of the major characteristics of modern civilization. Weber's work has its peculiar quality because it contains both his father's bourgeois political realism and his mother's evangelical crusading. His mother, as well as the rest of Weber's family background (hardworking business people), must have revealed to him in the flesh the connection between puritanical moralism and the nature of hardworking capitalism.

Similarly, the struggles over sexual freedom and sexual repression, as well as the rise of feminism and modernism, were not abstract intellectual issues for Weber. He was in the midst of them and paid a personal price. Out of this came his appreciation of the important personal dimensions of life, not only in the modern family and modern culture but, by extension, in his vision of societies throughout history. And the conflict between political careers and academic life, between action and reflection, gave him an aspect of both, and a detachment from both, that revealed their secrets as well as their weaknesses. Weber was truly in the crucible between contending forces, and his multisided intellectual work is the product.

One would also have to say that Weber had tremendous social advantages that helped make him intellectually successful. He knew the great intellectuals of his day, from his very childhood. The most eminent of the German historians and philosophers met at his father's house. During his university studies, Weber made a practice of hearing the lectures of all the most famous professors, even in fields removed from his own. This was no doubt one of the sources of his voluminous knowledge of world history, and of his sure sense of how to write on the level of masterpieces. The great historian Theodor Mommsen appeared at Max's defense of his doctoral dissertation, to name him as his own successor. Mommsen also was a family friend, and his son married Max's sister. Thus it was not surprising that the way should have been smoothed for Weber to acquire distinguished academic positions, even before he had published what we now consider to be his major works.

Weber was also lucky to have been in the company of his learned colleagues. Although he himself was a thinker of great originality, some of his ideas were taken from others. Weber made the doctrine of "ideal types" famous, but it was first used by a legal scholar, Georg Jellinek, who happened to be a colleague and a personal friend of Weber's at Heidelberg (Marianne Weber, 1926/1975: 314). In Weber's methodological writings, he was strongly influenced by his friend and colleague from the University of Freiberg, the philosopher Heinrich Rickert (who happened, incidentally, to be the son of another Berlin politician and friend of Weber's father). And the original concept of Weber's famous analysis of religious *charisma* was taken from Ernst Troeltsch, a Heidelberg theologian, who once shared apartments in the same house with Weber. In his intellectual circles, Weber was always face to face with the most up-to-date thinkers, which was certainly the best way of keeping himself in the center of modern thought.

Even the material conditions of intellectual productivity favored him. He regarded his editorship of the *Archiv für Sozialwissenschaft* as something of a duty and a burden, but it did provide him with a place where he could publish his own materials quickly and without passing any review. Unlike in today's journals, where authors may have to struggle for years with unfriendly referees, the academic journals of Weber's day were solely under the judgment of their editor; and Weber was the editor for his own writings. He felt no qualms about this, and even regarded it as his duty to keep the journal supplied with material. Similarly, his famous treatise *Economy and Society* was written to fill out a series under his own editorship, and was subject to no one's else's review. These were conditions of freedom and ease of publication that intellectuals of any period might well envy. And, in addition, Weber had the time. For over fifteen years—from his recovery from the depths of his illness when he began writing in 1903, until he again began university lecturing in 1918—Weber had almost no job obligations (except for his year and a half as a military hospital administrator at the beginning of World War I). He held no university position, and was not obligated to any duties except the editorial work he took on himself. Thus if he wrote some 4000 pages over this period, this only averages out to about 250 pages a year: an easy enough rate of production for a writer with no need to do anything but write.

On the whole, then, from the intellectual viewpoint, Weber's neurosis turned out to be almost ideal. Whatever the human price he paid for his freedom and his leisure, it is hard not to conclude that it ended up being worth it. And, given the way in which he finally moved himself toward a more liberated posture, one would like to believe that Weber would have seen it that way himself.

2

The Meaning of Ideas in History

Weber's Methodological Essays and Theory of Action

We have been introduced to Weber's intellectual split personality. On one side, there was the hard-nosed politician who possessed post-Marxian economic sophistication. On the other side, there was Weber the idealist, the thinker who gave ideas a dominant place in history. Most sociologists have a favorite side of Weber, but there is little doubt about which of the two is the more famous. Weber made his reputation on the basis of *The Protestant Ethic and the Spirit of Capitalism*, the book that turns Marx on his head. Instead of religious ideas being mere ideology, "the opiate of the masses" that reflects the material basis of capitalism, Weber shows that religious beliefs were themselves the basis for the emergence of capitalism. Added to this are the methodological essays Weber wrote at about the same time he wrote *The Protestant Ethic*. These contain his famous concepts of *verstehen* (understanding) as the correct sociological method, the use of *ideal types*, and his conception of society as the product of *meaningful human action*. All this is rather famous too, at least among sociologists, and it gives the impression that Weber is a kind of idealist hero: the man who showed that we cannot explain or even talk about the material world without invoking the subjective consciousness of human beings and the ideas they hold.

We will see later the actual extent to which this works itself out in Weber's sociology. In general, although he usually had the intention of keeping to this "idealist" program, he more often went straight into a rather materialist, conflict-oriented analysis of economic, political, and military conditions, and even gave the impression that ideas were determined by these conditions. But that is a subject for a later chapter. Weber seems to have generally ignored his methodology when he was actually studying sociology. The one exception is *The Protestant Ethic.* This makes sense, in terms of the actual pattern of his life work. As we have seen, Weber did virtually no intellectual work for over five years, after his breakdown in 1897-1898. When he finally began to recover in 1902, the first work he produced was a long methodological essay called *Roscher and Knies and the Logical Problem of Historical Economics.* This is his most important methodological work, and everything else he wrote later on this topic is an elaboration of what he says in that book. It was published in three parts between 1903 and 1906. In 1904, Weber took over the scholarly journal *Archiv für Sozialwissenschaft* and published as his first "editorial," an essay entitled "Objectivity in Social Science," which defends his doctrine of ideal types. During this time he was already working on his *Protestant Ethic* (which he began even before he found his ideas so strikingly confirmed in America), and which he published in the next two issues of the *Archiv* in 1904 and 1905. Finally, as it were placing the last bookend around *The Protestant Ethic,* he published his other famous methodological piece in the next issue of the journal (still 1905), "Critical Studies in the Logic of the Cultural Sciences," about what makes historical explanations meaningful. (These methodological pieces became famous in an English edition called *The Methodology of the Social Sciences;* Weber, 1949).

In other words, Weber seems to have had some personal need to work out these idealistic issues, at exactly the time he was beginning to recover from his breakdown. One could speculate that he had to come to terms with his mother's viewpoint of giving religion, idealism, and values their due; at the same time, he had to integrate them into his father's world of the harsh economic and political facts of history. Marianne Weber says that he struggled terribly in writing *Roscher and Knies*. This makes sense, if he was struggling not only to put his intellectual apparatus back in gear, but also to arrange a truce between the two warring principles of his background. For this period, at least, one would say that his mother's influence won: The Weber who has become most famous is his mother's son. But it was, after all, a compromise too, and Weber deals with how ideas operate in and upon the economic world of his father. Somehow this cleared his head, and as we get further away from this post-crisis time, Weber showed more and more flashes (some of them running to hundreds of pages) of sheer unadulterated materialism and *realpolitik*. To the end of his life, he never forgot his idealist principles, enunciated during 1903-1906, but he referred to them only intermittently, as if they had been something of which he had to remind himself continually.

Now, in a way, this biographical view is beside the point. The validity of Weber's ideas, on either the idealist or the materialist side, does not depend on the circumstances under which he formulated them. For this chapter, and, to some extent, in the next one, I will consider Weber mainly as "idealist." Let us see what the value of these ideas is in its own right.

WEBER AS IDEALIST

In what sense was Weber an "idealist"? Idealism has had a powerful effect upon German intellectual life ever since the great outbreak of idealist philosophies around 1780-1820, under the leadership of Kant, Fichte, Schelling, and Hegel. But there are different types of idealism; some of these Weber draws upon and defends, others he attacks.

(1) What might be called *epistemological idealism* comes from the doctrine of Immanuel Kant. Kant does not deny that the external world exists. But he calls it the "thing in itself," and he argues strongly that we can never know just what it is. For we always perceive the world through a screen of our subjective categories, mental forms that we place upon everything we might possibly see or even think about. Trying to see how things look apart from the forms through which we perceive them, is like trying to see what the world looks like when we are not looking at it. The attempt is self-contradictory. If we whirl around quickly to see how the

"thing in itself" really looks behind our backs, our categories have come along with us. It is like trying to see the back of one's own head—not in a mirror, but as it really is. It just can't be done.

Weber is a Kantian, or rather neo-Kantian, in exactly this sense. He believes that one never knows anything apart from the categories one applies to it. This applies to history, economics, current social life, and the individual human actor. All things one might know are seen through ideas. For the social scientist, Weber calls these *ideal types*. (Weber took the term from his friend and colleague, the philosopher Rickert, but it is Weber who made the concept famous.) Notice that for Weber (and for Kant), it is not a question of saying that the material world doesn't really exist, or that history didn't really happen. It's just that we can't ever know what it is in itself. History is an immense flow of particular events, spread out across millions of people and vast expanses of time and space. The social scientist is always selecting particular patterns to concentrate upon. And those patterns are framed by the categories of the observer's own analysis.

How "realistic," then, can such concepts be? Weber states that they are always idealized, in the sense that they are one-sided pictures, models of "pure types" that the world may approximate. But the world itself is a mixture of many kinds of things; hence ideal types have to be shaped so that they can be used in combinations. They are something like tweezers, to grasp historical reality somewhere between different tendencies. Thus "bureaucracy" is an ideal type, a form of organization in which everything is done according to the rules, everyone has a strict position, there is a clear chain of command, and so forth. Of course most organizations never really fit this model, and Weber is quite aware of it. Hence he pairs bureaucracy with another ideal type, "patrimonialism," which is a form of organization that is distinctly *unbureaucratic*, centered around personal networks and cliques. He can then characterize the history of various states as fluctuating somewhere between patrimonialism and bureaucracy (and of course various subtypes of these), and show the conditions that push it toward one end of the continuum or the other. History, in short, is an endless flux of particulars that we can never grasp in their entirety. But by using the device of ideal types, we can pin it down between certain fixed reference points, and actually propose a definite theory about how it has operated.

(2) *Historicist idealism* is a position associated with the philosophers Wilhelm Dilthey and Wilhelm Windelband, who wrote in the late 1800s Dilthey had divided the world of sciences into two realms: *Naturwissen-*

schaft or natural science, which comprises the sciences of inert or at least subhuman matter, such as physics, geology, and chemistry; and on the other hand is *Geisteswissenschaft,* the realm of the cultural or human sciences. On this side of the divide lies not only literature, but also history and social science. These concern the activities of human beings, who are alive, creative, and above all conscious. *Naturwissenschaft* can have general laws and be subject to causal explanations. *Geisteswissen-schaft,* on the other hand, deals only with the unique events of a historical flow of particulars. The aim of these sciences is not to produce general laws, but to interpret and understand the meaningful events that make up human history and human culture. Windelband called the two forms of knowledge *nomothetic* and *ideographic.* "Nomos," the Greek work for law or general principle, is the legitimate aim of natural science. "Ideo," however (Greek for "itself," implying the particular, as in "ideosyncratic"), tells us that the human realm is reserved for understanding and interpretation of each particular case, never for general laws.

Weber generally sympathized with this view of the world. For him, economics, history, and sociology are essentially "ideographic" disciplines. The aim is not to produce general laws, but to understand the meaning of particular events. The task of historical sociologists is not to give a general theory of revolutions, let us say, but to understand exactly why the French Revolution of 1789 happened as it did. But Weber is not as extreme as Dilthey and Windelband. For him, history and society are not merely an endless set of particulars, to be understood intuitively as if they were a work of art and the scholar an art critic. Weber uses his tool of ideal types to put at least some generality back into the process. He does not want to merely *interpret* history, but to say something about what *caused* it. To be sure, it is always particular things that we are explaining: Why did the French Revolution happen? Why did Western capitalism emerge? Ideal types thus not only tell us what categories, what kinds of "things" we are talking about; they also give us pictures, idealized models, of the causal connections by which things are brought about.

From the historicist camp of idealism, then, Weber brings away the conception that the human sciences, the *Geisteswissenschaften,* are always dealing with particulars, not with general laws. He does think, however, that we can impose our ideal types upon this endless flux. History may be a river into which one can never step twice, but through our ideal types we can impose some similarities on the places where we do step. More positively, Weber asserts that the appropriate method for the human sciences is *verstehen*, understanding. Because history is created by human beings, in order to explain it we must always project ourselves into the position of the people who created it, to see it through their eyes. *Geist*, after all, means "spirit," and to penetrate the nature of the *Geisteswissenschaften* we must get ourselves into the spirit of it.

(3) *Irrationalist or naturalist idealism* are terms sometimes used to refer to the philosophical tradition begun by Arthur Schopenhauer. A follower of Kant, Schopenhauer asserted that he knew what the thing in itself is: the will. We have not only ideas, the categories through which we see the world, but we also have our willpower, a blind (categoryless) force that pushes toward certain ends, the fulfillment of certain desires. The whole world, then, is made up of the dual entities, will and ideas. Schopenhauer had a powerful influence on such later thinkers as Nietzsche and Freud, who developed a more materialist version of will as virtually a biological force. This was not quite Weber's conception, but in many ways he is similar to Nietzsche, whom he spoke of as one of the two great thinkers with whom one must come to terms (the other being Marx). For Weber, the point is that society must be seen as the product of human wills. Individuals are not merely thinkers, philosophers with ideas (or ideal types): They are also actors. Furthermore, Weber stressed that the will is never reducible merely to ideas. Will puts an element of choice in the scheme. Hence human action is always directed toward ends (which Weber often spoke of as values or even "ideals"), but the choice of ends cannot be dictated by some kind of logic. This is the source of Weber's doctrine of the difference between "facts" and "values," of the inevitable choice that one always makes when one decides what to do. The social scientist, too, makes a choice of what ends to pursue, which is another reason why social science cannot be reduced merely to something dictated by "just the facts." The facts are of interest only from the point of view of some value, and hence do not speak for themselves. Weber is not, however, arguing for the use of social science merely to advance some political polemic. In fact, he says explicitly that political ends are only *one* value that a person might choose in studying social science; and he argued strongly that an interest in *scholarly* explanation is also an end in itself, and one that scholars ought to pursue.

Weber thus uses the conception of will, as separate from ideas, to found his doctrine of means versus ends, and of the free choice of ends. This leads him not only to a methodological view of the role of values in social science, but also to his theory of social action (which will be introduced below).

These are the types of idealism with which Weber was sympathetic. But there are other varieties of idealism, which he strongly rejected. For example, there is (4) *Hegelian or dialectical idealism*, which sees the history of the world as a logical unfolding of ideas. Weber was quite antagonistic to this view, which he regarded as a gross simplification of the actual complexities of history. He also rather strongly disbelieved in the assumption of progress, which Hegel (and his followers, such as Marx) saw as the long-term pattern in history. For Weber, history was much more like a tragedy, or a continual test of the human capacity to survive what it was doing to itself. Another type of idealism that Weber opposed was (5) *aesthetic idealism*. This is a position, made famous by Schelling and Goethe, in which the essence of the world is captured not by reason but by intuition. Recall that Kant showed we can never get to the thing in itself, because it is always masked by the categories through which we see it. Schelling proposed, however, that one could make a leap across the gulf, not by our ordinary rational and scientific concepts, but through art. For art gives an immediate intuition of what the world is really like, bypassing the problems of rationality.

This kind of aesthetic idealism had a powerful influence on nineteenth-century thinkers, particularly those who might be called the "romantics." The poetry of Coleridge, Keats, and Shelley was strongly influenced by this concept, as was the Amerian religious/philosophical movement called Transcendentalism. In social thought, this romanticist idealism was manifested, especially in Germany, in the belief that one could understand history as the manifestation of a certain spirit for each people, the so-called *Volksgeist*. Roman history was interpreted as the expression of the "spirit" or "genius" of the Roman people, just as German history or English history was a manifestation of their own Volksgeist. But Weber was very antagonistic to this kind of "explanation." It explained nothing, he argued, but only put a mystifying label upon what there was to explain. Aesthetic idealism offended his realistic sentiments as a social and economic historian. In addition, he disliked the conservative political connotations that usually clung to the conceptions of "the Nation" and its "national spirit."

Weber's methodological essays expounded his position in relation to these various kinds of idealism. There is more to it than that: He used Kantian epistemological idealism and historicist idealism to criticize "positivism," the position that social science can be reduced to just collecting the facts and formulating them as general laws. But as we've seen, Weber was not merely defending the role of ideas against a narrow-minded imitation of physical science. He was actually steering a middle course, trying to avoid as well the more extreme forms of idealism, Hegelian dialectics and aesthetic intuitionism, that he felt handed history over too easily to simplistic schemes and to subjective prejudices. Weber wanted a science of society. But it would have to be a science of historical change, and it would have to respect the endlessly flowing, complex nature of history, without reducing it to either absolute laws or to the realm of poetic intuitions. Instead, armed with his weapon of ideal types, he wanted the researcher to plunge into history as it really was, and to try to piece together what generalizations could actually be applied.

THE *METHODENSTREIT:* THE BATTLE OF METHODS

When Weber discussed these issues in his methodological writings, he was actually entering into the later stages of a debate that had been going on for twenty years. This was the so-called *Methodenstreit,* the battle of methods. It had started within the field of economics, which was at the time Weber's own academic discipline. The argument had broken out in 1883 between Gustav Schmoller, who was the leader of the "German school" of historical economics, and Karl Menger, then the most important Austrian economist. Menger is an important figure in the history of economics; along with Leon Walras in France and William Stanley Jevons in England, he had led the so-called marginalist revolution, which had ushered in the modern era in economics. Older economics, now called "classical economics," is represented by the theories of Adam Smith, David Ricardo, and others (including Karl Marx), which built the basic unit of analysis around the labor theory of value. "Neoclassical" or "marginalist" economics, which Menger and his contemporaries invented, substitutes instead the "marginal utility" conception of value, in which the value of anything on an economic marketplace is only relative to the amount of that thing that purchasers already possess. This is sometimes called a psychological conception of value, as opposed to the more objective value represented by labor power. The marginal utility theory allowed economics to be cast in mathematical equations, and has given rise to the mathematical theorems and proofs and the graphs that have dominated the discussion of economics ever since.

Schmoller was strongly opposed to Menger's marginal utility theory of economics, and to the entire "marginalist revolution" that created modern economics. This makes it seem that Schmoller was merely an academic conservative, holding onto the old ideas and refusing to go along with the times. But there is more to it than that. In Schmoller's view, Menger's economics was merely a more extreme version of a model that had always been wrong in the discipline of economics, even in its "classical" version. The German economists had generally been opposed to the economic theories of Smith, Ricardo, and others of the English and French schools. For the Germans, these theories were wrong because they tried to set up general laws, such as the law of supply and demand, as if they were eternally true, scientific principles. But such principles could not possibly be very general, the Germans pointed out, for supply and demand exist only where there is a market, and in fact markets exist only in certain, relatively recent types of society. The German economists, in other words, were historial economists. For them, the major problem of economics was to show the different types of economies that had existed in world history, and how one type changed into another.

Weber was very much a member of the German historical school of economics. The work for which he is most famous, his studies of the social bases of the origins of modern capitalism, is a typical topic for the historical school, even if he went far beyond them in originality and in the scope of his comparisons. Schmoller was the academic chief of German economics, and it was in Schmoller's own journal *(Schmoller's Jahrbuch)* that Weber published his first piece after his breakdown, in 1903-1906. Even the title of that piece, "Roscher and Knies and the Logical Problems of Historical Economics," reveals the tradition he was working in; Roscher and Knies were two of the major historial theorists of German economics who had tried to establish certain stages through which economies had developed. Furthermore, these might be called "institutional economists," because they were concerned not with the laws of the market, but with identifying the surrounding social institutions that determined whether and in what sense a market would exist at all. This, too, is what Weber devoted his life's work to; his whole sociology in a sense is nothing more than the institutional part of economics spinning free to become a field standing by itself.

But Weber, although fundamentally committed to the historical view, was nevertheless not entirely in sympathy with Schmoller and the historical school. Some of this we have already seen: for example, in his attack on intuitionist idealism, which posits that there is a certain spirit (*Volksgeist*) that is manifested in a historical period. In *Roscher and Knies*, Weber attacked those two representatives of his own historical tradition because their explanations rested too easily on this kind of *Volksgeist* explanation, instead of delving into the real complexity of material conditions and forms that made up various societies and their economies. Weber used his method of ideal types to steer a middle course, so that economics could deal with the complexities of historical reality, without losing hold on at least some set of causal mechanisms that could explain it.

In another respect, Weber was a good deal more sympathetic to Menger's marginal utility theory, and indeed to the classical English economics of the market, than he was to Schmoller and the German school. For although Weber agreed that the laws of supply and demand on the market were historically limited and not universal, he felt that the task of historical economics should be to show just how and under what institutional conditions this kind of market actually did emerge. For emerge it did; Weber believed that the appearance of this kind of market capitalism was the major event of modern times. Once it appeared, it did follow the laws that Menger and the others had established for it. Weber thus wanted to ground the neoclassical conception of the market on a historical and institutional foundation. (When he refers to the laws of the market economy, Weber usually refers to Austrian economist Eugen von Böhm-Bawerk, who was Menger's successor as the leader of the Austrian school.) For Weber, the neoclassical market is an ideal type; thus in a certain sense it is unreal and nonuniversal, just as the German historical school had charged. But because Weber believed history could be at least approximately understood by seeing it through the lens of ideal types, he effected a compromise that allowed both the neoclassical economic theory and the complexities of history to coexist, in the same scholarly universe.

There is one final reason for Weber's wish to compromise between the two warring schools of economics, the German historical school and the Austrian/English neoclassical school. Here, it comes down to a matter of Weber's personal politics. For the English (and after them the Austrian) schools were made up of typical nineteenth-century Liberals, believing in freedom of the market, laissez-faire, and minimal government interference. For them, capitalism was a good thing, and it ought to be left to develop unimpeded. This, too, was largely Weber's own political position, as well as the doctrine of his father's political party.

Weber was realistic and aware of the social costs and shortcomings of capitalism, but he honestly believed that it was superior to any other economic system because in the long run it was more productive. Hence Weber was drawn to the neoclassical viewpoint. On the other hand, Schmoller and the German historical school also formed part of his immediate political connections. Schmoller and other German economists in the 1870s had formed an association called the *Verein für Sozialpolitik*, the Unions for Social Policy. It held meetings to discuss academic research, and, more important, to publicize and lobby for application of their economic information in social reform. Weber belonged to the *Verein*, and in fact had begun his career by doing policy studies for it (on the Polish farmworkers question and other matters). But the policies of the Verein created a political strain for Weber personally. The Verein professors were what one today would call "reform liberals" (as opposed to the laissez-faire Liberals mentioned above), who advocated government regulation as the solution to most social and economic problems. Their popular nickname, in fact, was *"Kathedersozialisten"*—"socialists of the chair," or academic socialists. While the Marxists were pushing for socialism from below, via the workers and potential revolution, the Verein professors pushed for a paternalistic socialism from above. But this is exactly what Weber opposed; he always polemicized against bureaucratic control of the economy, which he believed would suffocate the goose that laid the golden eggs.

This gives us a last undertone in Weber's methodological arguments. Steering his way, as usual, between opposing positions, he attempted to work within the German historical camp in economics. But through his doctrine of ideal types, he made room for the neoclassical market economy, and tried to find the conditions that led up to it and made it possible. And his polemics on behalf of pure scholarship, and away from purely political applications of economics, were part of his concern that the reform politics of the Verein would not strangle the theory of capitalist society the way that government regulation itself, he felt, would strangle the market economy. Weber thus managed to pick a course between the two political poles of his personal background. In rejecting the Verein's pressure to engage constantly in ethically oriented government interference, he was lifting the burden from himself of his mother's constant moral injunctions. His doctrine of ideal types was the weapon that allowed him his freedom, by putting some detachment and scholarly objectivity between the activity of an intellectual like himself and the troubles of the world he was analyzing. It may well be that Weber had to make this intellectual breakthrough to get himself out of the paralysis of opposing forces that kept him from working for so many years.

WEBER'S ACTION THEORY

On the theoretical level, Weber applied his conceptions of ideal types and of *verstehen* to set up a model of how the human being acts. From his methodological arguments, he had arrived at the view that to explain something causally is for the analyst to put himself or herself in the place of the actor, to empathically share in his/her worldview and to understand the subjectively meaningful reasons for choosing to act as he/she did. Weber (1922/1968: 24-26) thus establishes a typology (a set of ideal types) of the various ways in which action can be oriented. These are described below.

(1) Instrumental or means/ends rationality *(Zweckrationalität)* is the type of action in which the actor is trying to accomplish something in the world by calculating how to arrive at some end. It is rational action, based on a view of how the world is organized, and what means are to be chosen to get to one's desired ends. It is the rational action of getting from A to B (or maybe from A to C via B, and so on). This is an important form of action for Weber, because it constitutes economic action at its highest, ideal-type level. Rational, modern capitalism consists of businesspersons making calculating choices of how to buy and sell, how to manufacture goods efficiently, all toward the ultimate aim of making a profit. Means-rationality also predominates in the archetypically modern form of organization, the bureaucracy. In a sense, all of Weber's historical sociology is set up to show the conditions under which this kind of social action emerges.

(2) Value-rationality, or *Wertrationalität,* is the type of action that is an end in itself. The action is not a means to an end, but itself embodies its own value. Weber had political and religious examples in mind. For instance, if a group of political demonstrators throw themselves against the police cordons of a government to protest an action they believe to be intrinsically evil, that is value-rationality: The demonstrators have made a choice that their protest is worth conducting, no matter what it costs them (for example, being beaten or sent to jail). They do not

calculate what would be the most effective way of getting rid of that government, which would be an instance of means-ends-rationality. Weber, incidentally, had a certain amount of sympathetic understanding of what such political movements were doing, though he himself always believed in taking the more calculating route of bringing about one's ends through political strategies rather than directly expressing one's values in a protest. He was sympathetic not just because his younger friends believed in this kind of politics, but also because he well knew that the means-ends route in politics does not always arrive at its result. There can be a long chain of causes and effects between A and B in politics (more like A to Z), and hence the action can easily be derailed and have no result at all. At least the political protestor gets to express his or her own values directly, even if his or her action is limited to protesting rather than changing the actual situation.

Weber also practiced a wider use of his category of value-rationality in his sociology of capitalism. In general, if modern capitalism was epitomized by means-ends-rationality, then value-rationality was one of the main obstacles against it coming into existence. In particular, the various world religions tended toward value-rationality. For a monk to devote himself to meditation is a deliberate choice, designed to achieve the goal of transcendence or salvation. But the act of meditation or prayer is a value in itself, and does not lead (usually) to any other actions that will change the world. Hence this is an obstacle to capitalism. I say usually, however, because Weber also figured out some hidden quirks of history, by which the value-rationality of certain religions led to means-ends-rationality of capitalism. We will see more of this in his *Protestant Ethic.*

(3) Emotional action and (4) traditional action are two more forms of human orientation toward the world. Weber puts them on a "lower" level, so to speak, than the two types of rationality, because they are not based on any conscious reflection, and because they do not operate to change the world. Emotional action is a direct expression of feelings, not even on the level of choice we find in a political protest or a religious prayer; it is on the level of crying when we are hurt. Sexual drives are another example of this for Weber. Emotional action of this sort enters into his sociological analysis mainly as something the higher forms of action have tried to control, as in the ways religion has opposed or regulated eroticism. Traditional action, similarly, is an obstacle to the rational development of the social world. It consists of doing things by habit, merely because they have been done that way many times before.

Weber treats traditional action, along with emotional action, as close to meaningless, and thus barely as "action" in the sociological sense at all: that is, action that can be understood by the empathic method of *verstehen*. Weber sees these as forms of action without a worldview and without choices. Nevertheless—and this is one of the ironies in Weber's theory—even rational action can become habitual, or "routinized." For Weber, the most important types of human action are highly meaningful, driven by ideas and ideals. And yet, they can easily fall off into merely habitual or emotional action, following well-worn grooves. Even rationality degenerates into tradition.

We will leave aside these ironies until we come to Weber's theory of rationality, in Chapter 4. How do the actions of individual actors go together to make up a society? For the most part, Weber has in mind some kind of structure, such as an economic marketplace, in which all the different actors meet and mutually relate their various means and ends. This really applies only to his concept of means-ends-rationality, perhaps to a lesser degree to value-rationality, although it is hard to imagine just how it fits with his other types, emotional and traditional action. But given this implicit limitation, Weber proposes that action is social where it takes other people into account: that is to say, the actor's world-view on which he/she calculates includes other people in it, in the forms of expectations of how other people are going to behave. The seller of some goods on the market asks for a certain price, because he/she expects that the purchaser will be ready to pay that price.

Weber has become famous in certain quarters of sociology because his action theory contains a very fluid element. The expectations that actors have of each other exist in that particular moment; they are not, Weber (1922/1968: 27) says, necessarily what is considered to be normatively "right" or realistically "accurate." The actors on different sides of the same transaction can have quite different subjective interpretations of what is going on, even though they may use the same ideas to define what they are doing. "Friendship," "love," "patriotism," "being faithful to a contract" can mean quite different things between a man and a woman, an officer and a foot-soldier, or a borrower and a lender. In other words, Weber implies that each actor can follow his or her own self-interest and see the interaction from his or her own vantage point.

Moreover, the interaction itself can be quite fleeting. Social institutions consist of nothing more than people interacting, and putting certain interpretations upon each other's behavior. What makes up the state is not some transcendental, eternally existing entity to which people must bow. The state is created by people interacting, and Weber (1922/1968: 27) says explicitly the state will no longer exist the moment people stop orienting toward it. This gives Weber a somewhat revolutionary tone, given that even the state is vulnerable to being socially redefined out of existence. If people's ideas create social institutions, then the institutions change when the ideas change. But most of the time this does not happen. Ideas seem to have a certain stability. (Or is it because, as Weber also has to admit, rational action can slide over into sheer habit? But he does not pursue this point into a theory of revolution versus stability.)

Social institutions, then, exist (according to Weber's exposition) as long as people hold the same orientations regarding the behavior they expect from each other. These expectations can be formulated as rules, maxims of how each expects others to act, which become part of everyone's worldview. Insofar as institutions are stable, it must be because this stability of expectations exists. I won't deny that there is a certain amount of ambiguity in Weber's theory here. There are two viewpoints on this theory in sociology, one stressing the way in which institutions depend on individuals and are vulnerable to multiple definitions of reality, and even to sudden revolutionary changes. This is Weber's conflict or reality-construction approach. There is another side, espoused especially by Talcott Parsons, which stresses the stability of expectations. In Parsons's formulation, action always (or almost always) takes place under a rule, a norm to which both partners are oriented. It is impossible to resolve the debate as to which position Weber really supports; both sides are considered in his writings. You must make up your own mind about which one you believe is most fruitful for your own view of sociological theory.

3

The Meaning of Ideas in History

The Protestant Ethic and the Spirit of Capitalism

We come now to Weber's most famous work. In fact, the fame of *The Protestant Ethic and the Spirit of Capitalism* is so great that it has obscured much of the rest of his sociology, especially the nonidealist aspect of his work. For many people, "the Weber thesis" is the argument that turned Marx on his head: Instead of capitalism causing religion, religion actually caused capitalism. There are many qualifications that we have to introduce into this. For one thing, Weber himself said that he was merely drawing out one side of the process, adding a factor that other people had overlooked to the more familiar material factors that brought about the rise of modern capitalism. It is silly to accuse Weber of being one-sided when he quite deliberately set out to do a kind of "ideal type" analysis, singling out religious ideas so that we could see their effects more clearly, apart from the other factors. His aim was to put it all back together later on, when we could see just how much of a contribution religious ideas make in comparison to all the other factors.

We should also bear in mind that *The Protestant Ethic* was Weber's first major writing on the subject of the origins of capitalism. He came back to the subject several times later in his career: in his "middle period" studies of the world religions (China, India, ancient Judaism), in his *Agrarian Sociology of Ancient Civilizations*, and again in his *General Economic History* and in his more encyclopedic writings. Each time he broadened his conception, even to what sort of religious ideas were important, In his middle period, for instance, it is no longer Protestantism in particular that is significant, but Christianity in general. Other writings fill in the model of material and political conditions as they interacted with religion and capitalism. This will be treated in Chapter 5.

THE PROTESTANT ETHIC

For now, the discussion will focus on Weber in his most idealist period, and with *The Protestant Ethic* as part of his concern to give ideas their due in history. This work is certainly an example of the method he laid out in his philosophical writings at this time. To understand capitalism, we must put ourselves into the place of the capitalist, to see the world from his point of view. (I am using the masculine pronoun here because Weber in fact was concerned only with the men of that time.)

Weber was concerned with the European world at the time of the Protestant Reformation. Martin Luther broke from the Catholic church in 1517. He abolished the monasteries, decreed that priests could be married, and translated the Bible from Latin into German so that the congregation could read it for themselves. His emphasis was on breaking down the power of the priest as a sole connection from ordinary people to God. Henceforth priests were to become as much like ordinary people as possible, and the people were to find their own access to God. Hence Protestants abolished the elaborate liturgy of Catholic worship, and substituted hymn-singing in which everyone participated. All these changes, Weber noted, made religion a much more powerful force in the world. There were no more religious "virtuosi," the monks, and even the priests were made more secular. The ordinary world was no longer considered a place without religious value, a place from which the religious person must escape. Instead, the ordinary world was the place in which everyone must work out his or her own salvation. Religion thus became potentially more powerful as a social motivation.

Luther's Reformation was adopted in many of the states of northern Europe. It spread mainly for political reasons, because Luther eliminated the power of the pope, and let each state establish its own church. This was welcomed, especially in Germany, Scandinavia, and England, where the local rulers had long been struggling for control of Church property and policy. In some places, such as France, there was a long struggle, culminating in civil war, between Protestant and Catholic factions, but with the Catholics eventually winning. In the south and in eastern Europe (such as Austria and Poland) the Catholics triumphed, and in the 1600s there was a long series of religious wars between the two sides. It is in this context that Weber saw religion as having a major effect in producing modern capitalism.

The Protestant churches split into various factions mainly as a result of the political situation. If each state could have its own church, then different forms were set up: an Anglican church in England, the Lutheran church in much of Germany (which at that time consisted of numerous small states with their own dukes or princes), and so on. In Switzerland, where there were many independent city-states, radical forms of Protestantism appeared, led by such reformers as Zwingli in Zurich and John Calvin in Geneva. It was their theologies, and particularly that of Calvin, that Weber believed had the greatest effect upon capitalism. There were also Protestant groups that were completely "private," in the sense that they were not supported by any state, for example, the Quakers and the Baptists. These groups tended to be "radical," placing such a heavy emphasis upon religious behavior that they often denied the authority of the state at all. (The Quakers, for example, were persecuted because they refused to submit to any kind of authority, including that of a Protestant minister, or even to take off their hats as a sign of respect to persons of higher rank.) These groups, which Weber referred to as "Pietist," made religious demands so all-encompassing that they threatened the social order. In the England of the 1630s and 1640s, they rose in rebellion (along with the forces of Parliament and some of the more "moderate" sects) and overthrew the monarchy and beheaded the King. And earlier, in Luther's own day (the 1520s), the German peasants were inspired by radical religious beliefs that the kingdom of heaven was about to be established on earth, and managed to organize a sort of mob-rebellion that was put down by the German princes. For this reason, Luther turned away from the more radical implications of his own Protestantism, and worked out a middle-of-the-road position, in which the church was allied to the state, and operated to maintain social obedience.

When Protestantism broke down the authority of the Catholic church, it opened the way for a variety of religious positions. Beliefs were no longer set forth as Catholic dogma and enforced by the Inquisition, with persecution for heresy as the price of holding the unorthodox view. To be sure, in the places where the Protestants came into political power, they too had a tendency to try to enforce their own theologies as dogma. But across Europe as a whole, there was a new openness of religious thought. This in itself created something of a mood of anxiety. It was a highly religious age, in which the church was present everywhere in everyday life, and going to sermons was even used as a source of entertainment (in the absence of much else). The afterlife, salvation or damnation, heaven or hell, were constantly drummed into people's ears. Hence the question of how to achieve salvation was an important one, especially because the orthodox view was made unsure by competing conceptions. This religious tension, Weber felt, was an important source of social motivation, as it made people strongly concerned to do whatever was necessary to save themselves.

In this situation, the most challenging theological position was that taken by the Calvinists. The doctrine was formulated by John Calvin in Geneva, but it spread across Europe especially in the Presbyterian church, which became politically important in Scotland, and in the revolutionary movement in England. The major point of Calvin's doctrine was predestination. Since God is all powerful and all knowing, there is nothing that He cannot do or know. God knows the entire past and the entire future, and by His power He has ordained everything that is to be. This implies that everything that everyone does is already predetermined. Whether one will be good or evil is determined, and so is whether one will go to heaven or hell. There is nothing anyone can do about it.

Naturally this caused a lot of anxiety among people for whom the tortures of hell were a vividly accepted reality. It did not help matters that Calvin declared we are all sinners, and hence all deserved to go to hell. Only the divine grace of God left a narrow escape route. God had preordained that some few, the so-called elect, had been chosen to be saved. It did not happen through anyone's actions or will; one could not buy one's way into heaven, by saying prayers, going to Mass, giving to charity, or buying indulgences, which were certificates sold by the pope to take time off from purgatory. Sociologically speaking, Calvin's extreme reaction against salvation by "good works" was largely an effort to negate all of the tactics of the Catholic church he was rebelling against. But the effect was that people believed only the sheer mercy of God could save anyone from hell.

Weber argued that this created an extreme condition of anxiety in any Calvinist believer. One was conscious of being a sinner, but terrified of hell and of the absolute impotence to do anything about saving oneself. The only chance one had was to be one of the elect, one of the lucky few whom God had picked. But how could you know whether you had been chosen or not? The only sign was to feel that divine grace had descended upon you. And—miraculously enough—such signs did come, and coincidentally only to those who believed and who belonged to the Calvinist group. If one was saved, however, it was not because of a choice one made at some point in life; the feeling of grace must have been there continuously. This created a motivation for the believer to try to make his or her life perfect in every way. Not just in religious matters (praying, going to worship) or even in moral purity (sexual puritanism, lack of indulgence in idle games and the like), but in every respect. Life was always serious, because it was a matter of knowing whether one was destined for heaven or hell.

The result of this religious doctrine, then, was to produce anxiety and a strong motivation to discipline one's life in every respect. The doctrine of predestination ended up producing hard work; one's whole life became a religious effort. Only by continuous, methodological work could the Puritan assure himself that he was saved. This especially motivated Puritans to go into business, in which one could put in long hours toward an endless goal of making money. Such a trade was better suited for the puritan life than agriculture, with its alternation of work and idleness dictated by the seasons, or the military and political career choices of the traditional upper class, with its conspicuous luxury.

The irony of this situation is that the Puritans became rich. Their long hours and methodological business practices led to the acquisition of wealth. Their businesses flourished; they became leading citizens. Capitalism grew, but puritanism began to fade away. The Protestant ethic, precisely because of its effects in transforming the world, eventually undermined itself.

CRITICISMS OF THE PROTESTANT ETHIC THESIS

Weber's theory very quickly became famous. It is easy to see why: Not only did it turn Marx on his head, and set forth a wholly unexpected connection between religious ideas and economic development, but its ironic conclusion also makes it a nicely dramatic tale. But is it true? A number of objections were soon put forward.

One counterattack expressed was the argument that radical Protestantism and capitalism are indeed connected, but that Weber had the order turned around. English historian R. H. Tawney (1938), for example, claimed that the reason the Protestant sects appeared in England during the 1500s and 1600s was precisely because England was beginning to undergo the capitalist revolution. Protestantism fits psychologically with capitalism, but the economy creates the ideas, not the reverse.

Other scholars (for example, Samuelsson, 1961) pointed out that Weber overstated the role of Protestant countries in the rise of capitalism. Belgium, for instance, was one of the important centers of modern industrialism, in fact it was the factory district of continental Europe in the 1800s (and still is). But Belgium is a Catholic country. The purpose of this argument is not to set up a rival "Catholic ethic" against the Protestant ethic, but rather to use the comparison to deny that religion really had anything to do with it. Instead, institutional and technical factors of economics brought about capitalism. England led the Industrial Revolution because it was especially favored by conditions of foreign trade, as well as by other purely material factors.

In recent years, yet another line of criticism has emerged. Scholars such as Lawrence Stone (1967) have argued that capitalism was not really produced by a "rising bourgeoisie" of small businessmen. The modest Puritan middle-class upon which Weber focused was not where the economic action really was. Instead, the aristocracy in England were the ones who were instrumental in developing capitalism by pushing the peasants off their lands so that they could convert them to sheep-grazing for the wool market; by digging mines for coal and iron on the country estates; even by setting up factories in the countryside, thereby evading the guild restrictions found in the cities. In this view, it was the "crisis of the aristocracy" that developed capitalism, rather than a Puritan bourgeoisie pushing upward from below.

WEBER'S DEFENSE

Many of these kinds of objections were voiced in Weber's own lifetime, although some he could not reply to because they developed after his death. But, to a large extent, Weber had already prepared his own defense. There has been a great deal of misunderstanding of just what Weber was stating. Not only do many scholars fail to realize that Weber published much more complex theories of capitalism after the Protestant ethic thesis, theories that fill in exactly the institutional economic factors that he is accused of leaving out. Even in *The Protestant Ethic* itself Weber stated that he was only spelling out one of many factors; he was conducting an ideal-type analysis, in the sense that he had isolated one "pure" condition for capitalism, that was in reality mixed with other conditions in the complexities of history.

More specifically, Weber was not bothered by much of the criticism because those who expressed it missed the point he was making. He was not arguing that *capitalism in general* was caused by Protestantism. He was drawing a connection between a particular kind of Protestantism (the Calvinistic belief in predestination) and a *particular kind of capitalism*. This is what he called "rational capitalism" or (more loosely) "modern capitalism." Capitalism, Weber says, has existed at many times and in many places. It existed among the merchants of ancient Bablyon, in India and China, and in the slave trade of the Roman empire. There were merchants with powerful guilds in the European Middle Ages. But none of these is representative of what he called "rational capitalism." This kind of capitalism does not merely consist of a market economy, the use of money, or the search for business profits. If greed were the main trait necessary for the development of modern capitalism, Weber declares, then there was plenty of that in the ancient world and in the Orient. But these places developed no capitalist "take-off," no industrial revolution that transformed the whole world into a vast business enterprise. Why not?

We can begin to see more of the charcteristics that make modern capitalism distinctive. It is large-scale: It is not just a few merchants here and there, little pockets in medieval cities, or a few ancient slave traders or oriental merchants of spices and luxuries. It must include everything, especially the banal necessities of life: food, clothing, simple household items. Traditional capitalism coexisted in a world where most households were relatively self-sufficient, where they grew their own food and made most of their own clothes and implements. Modern capitalism made all these commodities marketable; everything is bought at the store. Furthermore, modern capitalism is dynamic in a way that traditional capitalism never was. Medieval or oriental merchants sold the same kinds of goods in the same limited ways over many centuries;

markets rarely expanded, new goods were almost never invented and offered for sale. Modern capitalism, on the contrary, is constantly expanding. It has been characterized by a feverish search for new inventions, new methods of production, and new products to sell to consumers. It is the kind of capitalism we see all around us today, in which advertisements bombard us with new products, and businesses aggressively compete to expand their markets.

Now how did this mass-market, dynamic capitalism come into existence? The older kind of capitalism was essentially traditional and limited. Furthermore, Weber asserted, its very characteristics were obstacles to its further development. Take, for example, the greediness of the traditional merchant. He sold some luxury perhaps, brought at great expense and greater risk from a long distance. Spices from the Orient were a prime example in medieval Europe, though one could also name the trade in silk, or in tapestries, porcelain, or other fine goods. Because trade was risky, the merchant wanted to make as much profit as possible whenever he could. Business was a series of one-shot deals, episodes in which something was sold at the highest price possible. There was no thought of building up a steady clientele, because the next transaction would likely be in a very different place and under different circumstances, when the next ship came in from the Levant.

Modern capitalism, on the other hand, depends upon mass production and distribution. Mass markets are the essence of its operation, and these require regularity. Large quantities of goods must change hands in a predictable and repeatable way. Only in this way could the necessities of everyday life become items on the market. In order for this happen, one prerequisite was that the capitalist himself not be too greedy. He should cease to regard business as a form of gambling, in which one finally struck it rich all at once when his ship came in. Instead, modern capitalism called for capitalists who were satisfied with small profits, but repeated over many transactions. The secret is that much larger gains can be made in the long run by selling cheap items for a small but regular gain, than by making a large windfall profit on luxury goods sold at very irregular intervals. The businessman who makes a penny on each loaf of bread sold every day to millions of customers, ultimately builds a much larger business than the merchant who sells a rare diamond to an occasional few.

It is in this direction that the Protestant ethic has its economic effects in Weber's scheme. The Puritans were averse to the traditional form of capitalism, with its greed and gambling mentality. The Puritan wanted regularity, methodical work, day in and day out. Furthermore, the Puritan placed great emphasis on honesty; instead of cheating a customer whom he would never see again in order to squeeze out the highest price, he offered lower prices with small profits, decent quality, and honesty in dealing. No doubt (according to Weber) the motivation was purely religious. But the effect was that the Puritan businessman found himself with a clientele who kept coming back, who liked the way he did business. Weber quoted Benjamin Franklin (whom Weber believed stated the Protestant ethic very clearly in the 1700s when it was becoming secularized): "Honesty is the best policy." The Puritan may have started out being honest simply because that was part of his religious belief, motivated by worry about his own salvation. He ended up seeing that honesty was in fact a good policy, for purely business reasons. By this time, modern capitalism had taken off. Mass markets for everyday goods were expanding, driving out the subsistence households, and forcing everything into the realm of modern capitalism. By the 1800s, there was no turning back. The Protestant ethic could afford to fade away as a religion, because it had created an economic framework of modern society that now functioned on its own.

Puritanism contributed to the growth of capitalism in yet another way. Because the Puritan businessman was motivated by religious anxiety rather than by the search for gain, he did not feel he could simply consume his profits. The traditional merchant would have taken his good luck (when he had a success) and try to live the lifestyle of a noble lord; if possible, he would actually buy land and a title, and abandon business entirely. But the Puritan was opposed to licentious living, and was committed to his methodical enterprise in business. The logical thing for him to do, then, was simply to plow his profits back into the business. Karl Marx would later refer to this as the epitome of alienation: instead of money being used to buy goods that could be consumed, in modern capitalism money became simply a device to invest in making more money. There is no end to the chain. Marx thought this was the alienating nature of capitalism, while Weber saw it as the manifestation of a religious motivation that had very little to do with money at all. Business thus became an endless stream, fed by its own success, leading to the pursuit of endless growth.

In the chain of causes that produced modern capitalism, then, religious ideas played an important role. Actually, Weber identifies several points at which these ideas intruded. I have concentrated on the Calvinist doctrine of predestination and the way it produced feelings of

*Calvinist
hard work*

religious anxiety that were translated into continuous hard work, honesty, and the accumulation of small profits and their reinvestment in business. In addition to this particular doctrine of Calvinism more general Protestant doctrines played their parts. For Luther had stated the doctrine of the "vocation" or "calling." What this meant was that everyone was "called" to a particular station in life where their duty lay. This was part of Luther's elevation of the ordinary world into religious significance. Previously, only priests and monks were "called" to their professions. But Luther abolished monasteries and made priesthood just another vocation among others. In effect, all occupations now became roles to which people were called by the divine spirit. Work was given a positive valuation. For Luther, this had a somewhat conservative significance, given that he meant everyone should stay in his or her place; above all, the peasants should not rebel and try to overthrow their masters.

But Weber points out that the concept of the calling marks an important transition in social thought generally. In traditional societies, no one would have regarded work as having high value. For the religious elite, only prayer, meditation, and other full-time religious activities designed to get one *out* of the ordinary world had value; everything else was "worldly" in the negative sense. Not everyone was so religious, but the secular elite had a similar attitude. To the aristocratic lord who occupied a place at the top of the social hierarchy, work was considered drudgery, a sign of low status. Only slaves, serfs, and other low-born people worked continuously; everyone else devoted himself or herself to politics, to display, and to leisure as much as they could. Weber regarded this attitude as one of the main obstacles to creating a dynamic modern capitalism. The traditional attitude expressed was satisfaction with the world as it was, and the majority of people made no effort to change it. Luther's conception of the calling, in which every occupation now had its own religious dignity, its own positive significance, represented a major change in the status system. It dignified ordinary work, and thus paved the way for the more radical motivation in economic life that would ultimately change the world.

The Protestant concept of calling stands out by contrast to the Catholic attitudes that had prevailed in medieval Europe. Weber described the Catholics as divided into a religious elite—the monks—and the rest of the population. It was a religious two-class system. The monks alone were regarded as truly religious. They had cut all their ties to the world, giving up family, property, enjoyment, and career in order

*work and the
calling*

catholics - two class

to assure their salvation through continuous monastic discipline. We can see here the power of religion to create the strong motivations that order people's lives. But monasticism drained all the religious energy, so to speak, into an isolated sector, and away from society in general. Because the monks were so perfect, religiously speaking, the bulk of the population did not have to be. They could never reach the same level of perfection as the monks: They married and had sex lives, and they pursued wealth and power; in other words, they lived in the ordinary world. The only way they could be religious was in a second-hand fashion, by giving alms to the monks, and by receiving the sacraments of the priests.

Weber thus described the life of the rank-and-file Catholic as a cycle of sinning and repentance. One lived one's ordinary life, lusted and sinned, and then went to confession and to Mass, took holy communion, and was absolved of one's sins. The practice of buying indulgences in order to facilitate one's way into heaven was an extension of this attitude. (Remember that the Protestant Reformation was started by Luther's rejection of the sale of indulgences, which the popes had been resorting to more and more often to raise money.) Weber's point is that the Catholic religion was largely ceremonial rather than psychological and moral. It did not put very much pressure on ordinary people to live a religious life, because it was always possible to go to the priest, make a sincere repentance, and be absolved in return for receiving such ritual punishments as reciting hundreds of Hail Marys, or having to crawl up the steps of the cathedral on one's knees. Medieval religious life was full of this kind of public display of one's piety: Saints in particular were famous (sort of the "superstars" of the time, when there were no other forms of mass media) for the extremes to which they would go in making penitence for their sins—"mortifying the flesh" by whipping themselves, loading themselves down with chains, wearing hair shirts next to their skin, and so forth.

All this display of religion, however, was what Weber called "magical" rather than moral and psychological. It did nothing to transform everyday life in the working world, because it negated that world and regarded it as sinful. Religious actions instead were extraordinary, whether they took the extreme form of the self-abnegations of the monastic "heroes," or that of the ordinary person being forgiven for sins by participating in the rituals of the church. The medieval Catholic world was full of miracles, because this is what the magical emphasis of the religion valued. (Presumably the miracle stories that were so popular—seeing holy visions, bleeding from one's hands in the manner of Christ, the stigmata appearing on one's body—reflected the influence of psychosomatic processes, as well as magnification by rumor and self-aggrandizement, in an era when the social pressures of this kind of ritualistic religion were all-pervasive.) The emphasis on ritual and the search for miracles siphoned religious motivation away from any effects it might have had on transforming the world, and especially the economic world. The practice of Catholic religion, Weber argued, was thus an obstacle to the development of rational capitalism.

The importance of the Reformation was that it abolished this magical, ritualistic Christianity. At least it tried to, as elements of it survived, including in the Lutheran church itself: hence Weber's stress on the Calvinists, who were most opposed to ritual and magic. Perhaps this is why their doctrine stressed predestination: If God had fore-ordained everything that was to happen, then searching for miracles and doing penances would be fruitless. One could only be sure one was a member of the saved by being constantly righteous, not by sinning and repenting over and over again. Protestantism broke down the religious two-class system; it eliminated the monks, so that everyone would now have to be a kind of *monk within the world*. It eliminated as much as possible of the religious ritual, especially confession and penances, because they left too many escape hatches for sinners. Priests were no longer an elite, but married householders like everyone else; everyone had to be more or less his or her own priest.

Weber may have overdrawn his contrast between Catholics and Protestants. It would not be entirely fair to say that Catholics could sin as much as they pleased as long as they went to confession and did penances. The Catholic church did try to put moral and psychological pressure on its followers too. Particularly in the modern world, in the most recent centuries, Catholics have often been as intensely moral as Protestants, or even more so. And recent sociological studies find that in mid-twentieth-century United States, Catholics have become quite achievement-oriented, even outdoing Protestants in many respects. But these facts do not quite negate Weber's ideas. For one thing, Weber was dealing with the Middle Ages, when it was a question of whether rational capitalism would get going or not. In that situation, the relatively great emphasis of Catholicism on ritualism and the miracle-working "magic" of the elite of monks and priests can be seen as an obstacle to capitalism, and the Protestant Reformation had an important effect in changing that religious structure. Fifty years after the

Reformation the Catholic church launched the "Counter-Reformation," which was an attempt to clean up its own act, put more emphasis on moral behavior, eliminate many of the political abuses of the clergy, and in fact become a good deal more "Protestant" in its attitudes. (In fact one can see the Catholic church moving in a Protestant direction for several hundred years, most recently in the reforms that have eliminated Latin in the church service, brought more lay participation, and now are pressing toward allowing priests to marry.)

This is not so surprising for two reasons. One is that Catholicism and Protestantism are, after all, both branches of Christianity. In his later works, Weber was to place increasing emphasis on Christianity in general as the crucial background necessary for capitalism to emerge in the West, in comparison to Buddhism, Hinduism, Confucianism, and other religions in the East. Protestantism just added one last twist, one last incentive to get modern capitalism going. For this reason, as we shall see, Weber gave a lot of attention to ancient Judaism, the ancestor of Christianity. Judaism was very hostile to magical forms of religion, and Weber regarded this as an important step. *Entzauberung,* he called it, "taking the magic out." Protestantism, then, was a throwback to early Christianity, while medieval Catholicism was a temporary lapse back toward the magical side.

But once rational capitalism was under way, it pushed the "Protestant" world into dominance. Even Catholics had to go along with it. Indeed, everyone had to go along with it, even at the expense of one's religious beliefs. We have already noticed the irony that hardworking, methodical Puritans built up successful businesses, and in the process of becoming rich eventually become less religious. But the structure of rational capitalism is all around us, and we cannot escape from it. It is a world without magic, a world in which the hard forces of the market and the pressures of bureaucracy give a secular equivalent to individual powerlessness under God's predestination. Weber was pessimistic about the modern situation; he complained that we are caught in an iron cage of our own making. We are haunted, he said (1904-1905/1930: 182), by "the ghost of dead religious beliefs."

4

Rationalization

The Master Trend of History?

We are beginning to see that Weber's work is multilayered. Discovering his theories is something like peeling an onion, except that we cannot be sure which part is the core. Better to say he is like a diamond mine of unknown depth. What lies near the surface has been so glittering that it has attracted almost everyone's attention, distracting us from seeing what lies beneath. *The Protestant Ethic and the Spirit of Capitalism* set off immediate controversy, and has been known to this day in many parts of the intellectual world as "the Weber thesis." But even that acknowledgment has implied a focus on only the most surface-level aspect of his work, the theory that the doctrine of predestination caused Puritan Protestants rather than Catholics to develop capitalism. We have already seen that this is an oversimplification, that a deeper version of the "Protestant Ethic thesis" has more to do with the elimination of magic and ritual and the harnessing of religious motivations into the transformation of the ordinary world. The doctrine of predestination is not the most central part of the argument, and in his later works, Weber scarcely mentions it, even when he is talking about the Protestant Reformation.

But so far we have only been scratching the surface layers of Weber's work. More recently, some scholars have emphasized another layer,

which they claim is the real core of Weber's theories. This is the idea of
rationalization. We have already met this concept in the Protestant
Ethic debate. Recall that Weber was not arguing about the existence of
capitalism in general, which he notes has existed in many times and
places, but of *rational capitalism*. The idea of rationality goes beyond
capitalism, however. Bureaucracy can be considered the rational form
of organization, and in politics there is an ideal type of legitimacy that
Weber calls "rational-legal." His theory of action itself, as we have
already seen, is divided into different ideal types, including "means-
rationality" and "value-rationality." Hence it has been argued that
rationality is Weber's central concept, and rationalization is the master
trend of world history, especially in the development of Western society.
This position has been stated most strongly by the German scholars
Friedrich Tenbruck and Wolfgang Schluchter, following American
theorist Talcott Parsons (although Parsons made a less extreme
argument, allowing more qualifications, as nonrational processes always survived too).

But this raises an embarrassing question. What does Weber really
mean by "rationality" and "rationalization"? He frequently uses these
terms in one portion of his works (although at other times in his life,
especially when he was doing a very materialistically oriented analysis,
such as in *The Agrarian Sociology of Ancient Civilizations*, he did not
mention them at all), but he often used the terms without defining them;
and the instances in which he does define them give quite different
pictures. Let us see if we can figure out what the core meaning of
"rationality" is for Weber, and then answer the question of whether or
not "rationalization" really is the master trend of history.

SEVERAL MEANINGS OF RATIONALITY

(1) One meaning of rationality is found in Weber's theory of action.
Rationality consists of a relationship between means and ends, such that
the actor has chosen means that will actually lead to the consequences he
or she desires. Rationality here means technically adequate calculation
of how to get from point A to point B.

(2) When talking about world history, Weber often uses another
meaning of rationality. He frequently distinguishes rational capitalism
from traditional capitalism, on the grounds that the traditional form
was static, whereas rational capitalism was a major, world-transforming
force. Rationality here has the connotation of something active, a force

that masters the world rather than passively adapting to it or going along with a routine.

(3) A third meaning of rationality emerges as Weber compares different kinds of institutions. Bureaucracy is described as a rational form of administrative organization, as opposed to the irrational elements found in patrimonialism. Similarly, technology and science can be rational, as can a market system—but only under certain conditions. What conditions? The market is rational rather than irrational when it gives rise to predictable, regular setting of prices; above all when market relationships are determined by a system of accounting. The key here seems to be *predictability and regularity*. Thus law is rationalized when it is written, codified, and systematized by professional jurists. There is a strong implication that rationality is based on written rules, and hence on paperwork.

Are these forms of rationality all congruent with each other? They have some affinities, but they are not all the same thing. For instance, rationality as world-mastery does not necessarily follow from the definition of rationality as a correct calculation from means to ends, and neither of these necessarily implies rules codified in writing. There may be some historical connection among these, in that one may have contributed to another: in short, the "complex of definitions" may actually be a theory that certain things called "rationality" empirically caused certain other things also called "rationality." This is not a very good use of definitions, but at least we can see what Weber had in mind. But having made his clarification, we would have to admit that world-transforming, "rational" capitalism is only partly a consequence, *in Weber's own theory*, of either written rules or means-ends calculations. His full model, as we will see in Chapter 5, has many more factors than that.

It is better, then, to threat his various definitions of rationality as referring to three different things, which may become connected, but which can each have its own career. Now let us see if there is a historical trend for *any* of the meanings of rationality, so we can see if indeed rationalization is the master trend of world history.

RATIONALIZATION IN WESTERN MUSIC

Interestingly enough, Weber writes most explicitly about rationalization as the predominant historical trend not in his writings on capitalism, bureaucracy, or law, but in a little book he wrote in 1911 called *The Rational and Social Foundations of Music*. (The book was not published at the time, and appeared in 1921 only as an appendix to his encyclopedia volume *Economy and Society*.) The book appears to be unfinished, and ends without a real conclusion; but this style was in fact characteristic of much of Weber's writings. What is notable is that he analyzes the development of Western music repeatedly in terms of its increasing rationality, which separates it from the music of the rest of the world. Weber never defines rationality, however. We are left to discover what the term means from the way he uses it.

One thing is clear. Rationality here cannot have the same definitions as either of the first two meanings given above. Rationality in music is obviously not a world-transforming force; that meaning of rationality must be secondary and derivative. Nor does it make sense to say that rationality in music is a calculation of how to achieve certain ends by the proper use of means. Music is not a form of action in that sense at all. Only the third meaning of rationality might apply here, and we will indeed see that rules and paperwork do figure in Western music. But this is not the whole story; hence there must be a deeper meaning of rationality underlying the whole analysis.

What is distinctive about Western music? Westerners who have heard Indian sitar music, or traditional Chinese or Japanese music, recognize there is an obvious difference. But what does it consist of? Weber points out two main factors. First, the scale. The modern Western musical scale consists of twelve tones in an octave, which are then repeated at a higher or lower pitch. This seems "natural" to us, but in fact there are numerous ways an octave could be divided. Indian music theory prescribes 22 equal tones to the octave, the Arab scale has 17. On the other hand, ancient Greek and Chinese scales were "pentatonic," consisting of 5 notes, not reaching as far as the octave. (In fact, there were different kinds of pentatonic scales in Greece, depending on just which 5 intervals were chosen, the so-called Dorian, Phrygian, Lydian, and other modes; each of these had its own "feeling," and was reserved for particular kinds of religious or secular occasions.) A typical pentatonic scale can be produced by playing the 5 black keys in an octave on a piano. For Westerners, this gives a sound we regard as typically "Chinese," and this is often used as a theme in Western movies about the Orient.

What is rational about the 12-tone scale? Weber points out that these particular 12 tones were chosen (at least unconsciously) as the solution to a problem. The problem is a central one for musical harmony. The octave is "natural," in the sense that human ears universally hear a high C as the same as a middle C and a low C. Once one gets to the next octave up or down, the melody can repeat. Notes an octave apart sound congruent with each other. There are a few other intervals that have some of this quality: the so-called 4th (F in a C scale) and 5th (G in a C scale). Chords can be built upon these notes (especially by adding a third note, so that we get a C chord C-E-G, an F chord F-A-C, and a G chord G-B-D). But this depends on dividing the octave in such a way that the distance between the notes is just right for these harmonious chords. The relationship between C and F, and that between C and G, is natural, so to speak; but to fill in the full chords, one must decide where to place D, E, A, and B. Furthermore, if this is done in a certain way, the musician can modulate through a cycle of chords. The G chord (especially when the seventh tone is added, G-B-D-F) has a tendency to resolve into a C chord: in the sense that the ear finds it "natural" for one set of notes to be followed by the other. But the D-7th chord resolves into G, the A-7th into D, and so forth, making a cycle in which any chord can progress all the way around the various keys and finally arrive back where it began.

Western music since the 1500s has been based upon this chord system. Our melodies play around the chords, following the notes of a chord and the way one chord leads the ear to another; tunes also take their "direction" from weaving in certain dissonances that nevertheless take their musical power from the underlying chord system they are played against, because they lead the ear to expect a movement back to the chords on which they resolve. Most of our music is based on this structure, from Bach and Mozart to rock and jazz, though it is played with different instruments, different rhythms, and different amounts of noise. By contrast, the melodies of Indian ragas sound alien because they are not based on a chordal system, and because their scale does not recognize the Western 12 tones but instead plays on a much more finely graded set of tones. Even more remote from us are the pentatonic melodies of the Chinese or the ancient Greeks.

A second factor distinguishing Western music is its emphasis on polyvocality. Most ancient and non-Western music has a single voice; if there is more than one single instrument, they play the same tones in unison or just octaves apart. Or one instrument might constantly play the same note as a base drone (as in many Indian ragas), while another instrument or the singer weaves a melody above it. But it is fairly distinctive to the West to have several different voices going at once, each carrying its own melody, and relating the melodies to each other by principles of harmony.

Now polyvocality, Weber points out, is a social innovation. It makes music playing into an organization, and sometimes a rather large one.

The Western orchestra is a large musical organization, virtually unknown anywhere in the world before Europe developed polyvocality in the 1400s A.D.; and the orchestra took several hundred years after this to evolve to its modern size. In some sense, Western music is more "bureaucratic." There are more distinct roles for musicians, and they need to be coordinated into a combined product. Hence another precondition for the rise of this type of music was a system of measuring time as a fixed series of beats, with notes of standardized lengths, so that all the musicians could keep their different melody lines coordinated. Interestingly, the written notation system that could do this appeared long before polyvocality. The written staff, with its horizontal lines to represent where notes would fall, was developed in European monasteries in the 800s A.D., and was divided into time measures in the High Middle Ages, the 1100s. The 12-tone scale was evolving too, so that finally by the 1500s all the elements of "Western" music were in place. From this point onward, we are in the presence of music that is recognizable to modern ears.

Another social consequence of music being written down in a formal way is that for the first time in history, composers are well known as individuals. Ancient and oriental societies usually had anonymous musicians; compositions might be improvised and then copied by disciples. But this structure was relatively traditional, and the same tunes and styles of playing could be carried down from great antiquity: in fact, in India and China the prestige of the music often depended on how old it was and how faithfully it was reproduced. The West, instead, takes a turn toward the composer as a "creator," eventually developing into the cult of musical "genius" that centered on such figures as Beethoven and Wagner, and that still survives around the flamboyant popular musicians of today. Western music becomes dynamic, in the sense that it deliberately creates its own history. Composers write down their compositions and want personal credit for them. They become famous names. By the same token, they become ideals for later musicians to live up to and to surpass, by creating still newer forms of music. The peculiar "creativity" of Western music is thus socially based.

What does the history of music tell us, then, about the meaning of rationality? Obviously it is not merely characteristic of capitalism. The items in musical history that Weber considers to be crucial steps in its rationalization go back as far as the 800s A.D., long before there was capitalism, not to mention bureaucratization, or other institutional transformations. Music shows us a deeper root of rationality. We have already seen that means-ends rationality also does not apply. But what about the notion that elements of the world are fixed and predictable, and organized according to explicit rules? This seems to be part of it. The rise of the 12-tone system and its chords, and the written staff and notation for expressing it on paper, was indeed a development of a system that was fixed, publicly available in records, and from which certain predictable patterns followed. An analogy exists between music and capitalism, in the sense that when a fixed system was established, it could be used to run through many permutations, and hence could give rise to new forms of social creativity. Both music and capitalism could become dynamic and in a metaphorical sense "world transforming" once they were rationalized. This also meant that a more complex form of social coordination was built into them. The orchestra and the corporation are in a certain sense parallel. Similarly the new-style composer, competing with rivals and predecessors to acquire fame by innovations, is a kind of business entrepreneur in the realm of music.

But what are the sources of this development? The fact that rationalization in music precedes that found in capitalism by a long time is striking; it means that music is not an offshoot of capitalism—and it seems absurd to claim that causality went the other way around. It would be more reasonable to say that Weber is sketching processes that can occur separately, in different spheres of life, that need have no connection with each other, and that can each go their own way.

In fact, Weber does describe some of the steps by which the characteristics of "rational" music were attained. But there is no steady trend in this direction. An important early step, he argues, was to standardize or fix any notes at all, to move beyond a random collection of sounds that someone might make on different occasions. The same notes had to be recognized, remembered, and reproduced. This happened already in tribal societies under the influence of magic. Magicans singled out certain musical patterns, and fixed them as formulae for producing certain magical effects. This magical, and later religious, use of music was predominant also in ancient civilizations such as China and Greece. Weber regarded it as a step toward rationalization. But there is an irony here. The step was in a "rational" direction, but it stopped halfway. Magical music was rational insofar as it led to standardization, but "irrational" in that it stereotyped music into certain formulae, beyond which one could not go.

For Weber, this is not just a curious fact. It is emblematic of a problem with rationality throughout. Insofar as rationality is the creation of fixed rules, it may enhance the capacity for social coordination and hence for creativity; but by the same token, the very fixity of the rules can be an obstacle to creativity, to moving beyond the point already attained. Weber had the same attitude about bureaucracy: At some points it played a creative role in transforming the world, but in the twentieth century he had come to see it as a menace to the continued dynamism of the West. Too much rationality is not a "good thing." Weber always pointed to halfway as better.

The same applies to later steps in the development of modern music. Writing systems, the notation for sounds and times, and the musical staff were all indeed steps toward the flexible coordination of musical voices in a harmonic system. But Weber points out that systems for writing music did not exist only in medieval and modern Europe. The ancient Greeks developed their own notation, although it served mainly to describe their pentatonic system, rather than to move toward a 12-tone system. Weber does mention in passing, though he does not elaborate on the case, that at one point in classical Athens, musical forms did become more innovative, much to the consternation of conservatives who regarded these innovations as sacrilegious. This was also the time when musical theory was being written down by the Greeks, and the one instance in which composers are known by name. But somehow the development was derailed. There is room here for an important contribution in the comparative sociology of music, if someone were to investigate this case.

So it seems to make a difference, not just that there be a written notation system for music, but that it be used in a certain way. Arab musicians in the Middle Ages also had a notation system, and they developed their musical theory as well as their practice. Arab music at this time was not static. It did not go toward the 12-tone harmonic system, however, but elaborated new intervals until it arrived at a 17-tone system. Weber regarded these intervals as "irrational," because they could not be used for building a system of chords that provided a dynamic underpinning for melodies, for modulation from one key to another, and the other characteristics of the takeoff of Western music. Weber here seems to imply that there was actually a "scientific" problem of how this structure of acoustics could be solved. But it is hardly plausible that European musicians of the Middle Ages were consciously trying to create a kind of music they had never heard, and that would emerge fully only centuries in the future. It sounds more like the "natural selection" of a particular musical form, which, when hit upon, made possible this kind of creativity in the realms of chordal harmonies and melodies.

Arab music, on the other hand, moved steadily further away from chordal music, because the more intervals that were recognized within the octave, the less composers were able to build a chordal system upon them. So history shows instances of trends toward what Weber regarded as irrationality rather than toward rationality. Furthermore, this "irrational" trend was the product, not of some primitive social institutions, but of relatively rational ones. Arab musicians had become organized as a profession, rather than as amateurs, and had established their own technical standards and systems of knowledge in which novices were trained. In fact, it was precisely the "virtuoso" attitude that professionalism cultivated that caused the Arab musicians to embark on the invention of additional intervals. This was a creative development, moving far beyond the old Greek pentatonic scales. Weber describes it as the movement of these proud virtuosos, deliberately breaking the rules in order to show off their musical superiority. The pattern is parallel to Western composers of the last few centuries, who have constantly broken older rules in order to establish new forms. In the case of the Arabs, however, Weber regarded this development as irrational.

Is there a way to reconcile these varying positions? Are we simply dealing with a confusion that Weber himself had, over the meaning of the word "rationality"? I will admit that Weber does not seem to have worked over his vocabulary systematically, but I think that nevertheless he was consistent on a deeper level. Our mistake is to regard rationality as some kind of constant thing, which steadily evolves over time. Weber gives us a rather different picture. Rationality is a complex of factors that does involve calculability, formal and fixed rules, written notations, social coordination, intellectual systematization, and profession-alization. But each of these elements is a two-edged sword. Taken by itself, each one can advance the amount of creativity and accomplishment in a society, whether musical or economic or political. But if left to itself, each separate factor will produce results that diminish creativity and world-transforming capacities in the long run, whether by producing stagnation in a fixed position or going overboard in the opposite direction of pure idiosyncratic, personal accomplishments that undermine any social pattern. It is only when the various elements are balanced, in a situation of conflict or tension against each other, that there is a continuing trend toward rationalization, in the largest sense.

RATIONALIZATION AS SOCIAL TENSION

Weber himself explicity stated a view of rationalization as consisting of a set of tensions or conflicts. In 1915, when he was publishing his studies of world religions, he interpolated between his studies of China and of India a short essay called "Religious Rejections of the World." He described the essay as a contribution to the "typology and sociology of rationalism," in other words, a brief description of the most rational forms the social world can take. Here he does define rationality; he says he is using the term in "the sense of logical or teleological consistency" (1946: 324). In other words, human beings have a drive to be consistent, to draw out the logical deductions from any particular postulates or worldview. Part of what he is concerned with here is intellectual consistency, because he is developing a typology of religious worldviews and their consequences. But in addition to the "intellectual-theoretical" realm there is also the "practical-ethical," action as well as thought. There can be rationality (or irrationality) in either realm, depending on how consistently the consequences are drawn out from a given starting point.

Weber is very well aware that the entire world is not rational in this sense. He states that he is dealing with ideal types, that is, with particular elements that make up reality. Religious ideas have consequences for behavior, and that is what he is tracing here; but he also recognizes that religions are subject to forces other than intellectual ones, and that they might integrate ethical postulates, for example, that can't rationally be deduced from their own central intellectual premises. Weber is saying there is a drive for rational consistency, but this is only one force in the world among others. Part of the drama of world history is the way in which these forces interact with each other.

This definition of rationality given by Weber does not solve all the problems I have raised above. It is one element of the "family of meanings" that Weber gave to the term. It does not exactly explain how Western music can be rational, for instance, because one would not say that music involves the deduction of consequences from a given starting point. It would be more accurate to describe Weber's essay on music as drawing out the *unintended* consequences from a particular formal set of musical tones and rules that Western music happened to have hit upon. Furthermore, in this same essay on "Religious Rejections of the World," Weber begins to use the term "rationality" in several of the ways identified earlier in this chapter. When dividing religions between asceticism and mysticism, he chooses a type of "rationally active asceticism," which "in mastering the world, seeks to tame what is creatural and wicked through work in a worldly vocation" (1946: 325). He has in mind here the Protestant ethic type of religious self-control and self-denial, which has as its unintended consequence the transformation of the world. The mystical type is the opposite, an escape from the world; but Weber describes it as using mystical contemplation for "grasping of the ultimate and completely irrational meaning though mystical experience" (1946: 326). It's not just consistent logical deduction of consequences that is rational, but mastering of the world; on the other hand, the sheer transcendent experience of the holy itself is irrational. I don't think either of these follow from Weber's definition of rational as a consistent logical deduction. But let it pass: Weber has a message to give, and these words are his tools, even if we have to distinguish among the various meanings he gave to them.

One important point to note is that anything at all can be rationalized (in the first sense, of being consistently deduced). Mysticism itself, as a form of religious action, can be quite rational, even though Weber declares that its end experience is not. He says that the religions of India are the most rationalized expression of the abnegation of the world. That is, once fleeing from the world is taken as a basic postulate, the Indian religions (Hinduism and Buddhism) are its most consistent, thorough development. Obviously this kind of rationalization is very different from the rationalization of the Western, activist religions (Judaism, Christianity, Islam). But both are equally rationalized, carrying through on their own postulates; it is just that they start from different postulates. This is one reason, as we shall see, that different forms of rationality can come into conflict with each other.

In fact, as Weber (1946: 328) says, the more rationalized different spheres become, the worse the conflict grows between them, for rationalization makes people conscious of the "internal and lawful autonomy" of each sphere in its own right. Every institution has its own logic, and as these are more deliberately worked out, formulated into explicit rules and principles, the divergence among them becomes more apparent. Weber proceeds to illustrate the point by going through a series of ways in which religion conflicts with other institutions.

Part of the systematic development of religions occurs when the original magic conception of the holy is developed by a prophet or savior's commandments into an all-encompassing way of life. Instead of transitory, momentary experiences of spiritual force such as happens in primitive magic, the believer is now given the goal of finding a permanent state of salvation. This is the guiding idea of a rationalized religion; the corresponding phenomenon in the realm of conduct is that one's whole life, not just small parts of it, must become organized for religious ends. Religion becomes a total worldview and a total guiding force. For this reason, rationalized religion comes into conflict with other institutions, which it slightingly refers to as "the world." The world is merely "worldly," something to be overcome, or at least to be put in second place.

The first conflict is religion versus the family. In the agrarian societies within which world religions arose, the family (household and kinship) system was the basic form of social organization; it was where people lived and (generally speaking) worked, and where their primary loyalties were supposed to lie. Religions challenged this. The charismatic religious leaders all enunciated something like Jesus' admonition that his true believers should put their families behind them and follow him. This was especially so in the monastic religions, which called upon their converts to become "dead to the world," to give up all their possessions and enter the cloister or the life of a wandering alms-seeker. But it was also true that priests, as well as monks, were usually supposed to be celibate, in order to break the tie to the family. In the long run, Weber was to emphasize, this breaking away from the family-based society was to have major consequences for social transformation; it created new forms of organization and new levels of motivation that could eventually overturn the traditional society circumscribed by kinship. But initially this took the form of a conflict. Leaving one's parents and even one's wife and children, as the world religions encouraged individuals to do, was obviously an act of disloyalty to the family. It was proclaimed in the name of a higher ethical system, but nevertheless it was a blow to the ethical demands of the family group. From the beginning, rationalized religion came into conflict with the institutions of the world around it.

From Weber's point of view one would not say this is a conflict between two rival forms of rationalized organization; the religion was rationalized, but the family was merely a traditional form. This did not make the conflict any less real, though Weber implies it was less acute than what was to come later. A second and more significant conflict occurred when the economy became rationalized. Rationalized religion, at least of a specific kind, was one of the causes of this development;

asceticism in the world, as developed especially by Christianity, helped produce capitalism, and not just any capitalism, but rational capitalism. Here Weber describes the rationality of capitalism as a form of the market economy in which all the factors of production move freely on the market and are subject to calculation by business entrepreneurs. Economic rationality here means that the market follows its own impersonal laws. It follows its own dynamic, unimpeded by any other forces. Hence individuals must go with the market; laborers must move around to find the place that will pay the most for their labor, and capitalists invest their money where it will bring the greatest profit: both sides are compelled to do so because if they do not they will be destroyed by the market.

Weber thus credits the rationalized market economy with a great dynamism. Like any other institutional sphere that has become rationalized, it becomes an impersonal order with its own laws. Parallel to this, the salvation religions have depersonalized the holy. There are no longer merely local gods, glorified human beings looking after special groups of followers, but only one almighty God, Allah, Brahman, or an even more depersonalized condition of Nirvana or Tao. It becomes sacrilegious to reduce the holy to the level of a mere person (though religions of course vary somewhat in the amount of personification they let in). The most extreme and consistently rationalized religions, in Weber's view, are those that make the power of God absolute, and hence that push toward predestination or some absolute mystical level of unknowability. In either case, the holy is far from the earth, and so powerful that humans cannot control it or propitiate it; they can only bow to it, or try to merge mystically with it.

Here we come to a central irony, or perhaps dialectic, in Weber's view of the relationship between religion and capitalism. The earlier view expressed in *The Protestant Ethic* is only one small part of the story. Religion does not simply produce capitalism; it is also in opposition to capitalism. He points out that monasteries, for example, almost always become wealthy over a period of time. They have certain built-in advantages over secular society: Because their members don't own wealth, it is all saved, hoarded by the organization. As objects of veneration, they are given gifts by the surrounding society, but they don't give out material expenditure in return. They become property owners. The disciplined life called for by religion is often put to work, hence monasteries (in medieval Europe, in China, and elswhere) became centers of rationalized farming, production, and trade. Their wealth and reliability made monks into bankers for the surrounding communities. The consequences are the same as those of the Protestant ethic, which made its followers rich.

But wordly success comes into direct contradiction with the original religious ethic that made it possible. The religion is supposed to be avoiding the things of the world, and instead it becomes loaded down with them. Churches become tied to secular affairs. Furthermore, they become part of the social and economic elite, and tend to become a conservative force, part of the "establishment." This contradicts the basic ethical tenet of any universalistic religion, which is basically the feeling of the brotherhood of all humanity. Spiritual equality conflicts with the worldly success of the church. This often has led to conflicts within the church itself, in the reform movements that have been characteristic throughout many centuries of religious history. (We still find them today, in conflicts between the liberal-humanitarian and the conservative sides of the Catholic church, as well as in the Protestant denominations.)

Even more important, a rationalized religion feels a basic ethical conflict with the world of capitalism. From the point of view of religious ethics, the domination of the market and its impersonal values are the negation of the injunction to "love thy neighbor," or to pursue holiness rather than the things of the world. The Catholic church of the Middle Ages, although it prepared the way for capitalism, also was an enemy of capitalism. Its canon law prohibited the making of loans for interest, because this was usury, benefiting from someone else's misfortune. Weber pointed out that this was irrational from the point of view of the development of the capitalist market, because it impeded the flows of capital and the rational effects of investment. But what was irrational from the point of view of capitalism was rational from the point of view of the values of the church. Similarly, its sermons admonished good Christians not to be greedy, to pursue spiritual goods and not worldly ones. This was consistent with religious values, and hence rational in its own sphere.

We can see now that in Weber's view rationality is not a simple "progressive" force in world history. In fact, he believes that tension causes social changes. Continuous efforts to achieve consistency in turn give rise to new tensions. Weber suggests that there are only two completely consistent solutions to the problem of religious brotherhood versus the tendency of religious asceticism to create riches and hence ensnare one in the materialism of the world. One is the concept of the calling, the religious conception of the vocation that declares it is one's religious duty to carry out one's normal duties in the world. This was of course prominent in Protestantism (although it can also be found in Islam, and indeed in the argument of some of Hindu religion that it is one's religious duty to carry out the work of one's caste). This solution avoids the contradiction between the ethics of brotherhood and the self-interest of the world by giving up brotherhood.

Weber thinks this is a consistent solution, but I'm not so sure. The Protestant conception of the calling, at any rate, is historically unstable. As Weber himself says, it leads to worldly success, and eventually to latter-day Protestants becoming secular and unreligious. One could say it is a halfway house to the dissolution of religious worldviews and imperatives. The core of any religion is always the community of believers, and without this social element it ceases to be religious. Furthermore, religious congregations have survived in the modern world, if often in an increasingly sectarian fashion; but all of them in their way are concerned with ethical questions applicable to everyone. Liberal religions uphold the brotherhood of man, and continue to be hostile to capitalism, or at least try to mitigate its damages. Conservative religions deny the value of worldly ends entirely, and continue to uphold transcendental values in their place.

The other solution to the contradiction between brotherhood and worldly success, Weber says, is sheer mysticism, which radically denies any activity in the world. Both of these solutions, the religiously legitimated worldly vocation and the mystical world abnegation, are rational; on those grounds, there is no historical pressure toward either one. But mystical religion has its own contradictions, for the more rationalized and consistent the mysticism is, the more it calls upon true believers to retire from the world and become monks. Of course not everyone can do this; some people have to work, if only because the monks themselves need to be fed. And of course some people must continue to have families and propagate if there are to be any more monks. Monasticism implicitly needs the world, even if just to stand outside of it. Hence monastic religions turn into a "religious aristocracy." If only the pure meditators achieve holiness, then the world is divided into the religious elite and the masses. The latter are inevitably religious second-class citizens. This is so even if the religion isn't monastic, if the meditators try to live on their own resources. Nevertheless, they cannot avoid a "holier than thou" attitude, precisely because they are withdrawing from the ordinary social world and its concerns. But this offends the basic principle of any universalistic religion: the ultimate spiritual equality of all people. Mystics begin to appear as selfish, concerned only with their own salvation. No one feels this more strongly than the mystics themselves if they have full religious sense. Hence mystical religions always tend to deviate from their own foundations, and to proselytize. Buddhism, although it aimed to withdraw rationally from the world into an ordered life of meditation, felt the need to extend salvation to others. The result was that its monks became more involved in the world; Mahayana religion evolved into something rather like a popular salvation cult, complete with popular gods (and hence economically thriving temples). Similar patterns have occurred in other mystical religions. The forces of rationality in religion press in opposite directions on certain inevitable dilemmas; and each form of rational, consistent development of a particular point of view leads to contradictions and hence to changes.

The tensions do not end here. Religion is not only in conflict with the rationalized economy (though also supporting it) and within itself, it also has a similar relationship with the state. Weber points out that the state is based upon violence. Force is the specific means it uses to enforce social order and to exercise power. But force has its own logic: namely, to win, using whatever tactics are most appropriate militarily. Weber declares that this is inevitable, that even a peaceful state must be prepared to defend itself. Furthermore, the prosperity of a state depends on its power, and economic groups—and religious ones as well—are relying upon the state to underpin them, whether they admit it or not. The more rationalized the state becomes, the more its members become aware of their own specific institutional interests and the technical issues of how to exercise power. The rational state, in Weber's view, leads to the outlook of *realpolitik,* seeing the world as a lineup of military forces that have to be dealt with on their own terms. Similarly, inside the state, political maneuvering takes the form of making alliances and changing them at opportune moments; it is a conflict of factions, in which the underlying rule is that loyalty is always provisional, and principles cannot get in the way of acquiring power and holding on to it. Political and military realism is the underlying principle that rationalized states and their leaders must adhere to if they are to survive.

This comes into direct conflict, however, with the religious position. Not only is the state basically worldly, but it is fundamentally unethical. This is irremediable; the power politics of states cannot be done away with, and religious or other idealists who try to deny the realities of power are themselves always swept away by it. (That is, either they fail to change the world, because they lack the power, or they become organized as a religious/political movement, in which case they inevitably become entangled in the realities of power politics themselves.) The history of Islam, a conquering warrior religion, is just one example of this. The same conclusion is proved by the innumerable instances in which Christianity became a theocracy, a state church, or even just a militant sect intervening in politics.

There is an inevitable conflict between the rationality of power politics and the side of religion that tries to uphold ethical principles. This conflict arises most acutely when both sides are most rationalized, when they have developed their own bureaucratic organizations and their own "house intellectuals." Of course there are various efforts at compromise. States have often sought religious legitimation, and churches have usually welcomed the support of the state. This has usually meant that the churches themselves have diluted their ethical beliefs in order to retain power. Ethical beliefs have been especially vulnerable in times of conflict between rival religions, because then the temptation to use the power of the state to suppress one's rivals is overwhelming. Religious persecution has always been organized at the instigation of one religion against another, whether it was the Roman state cult persecuting the early Christians, the later Christians persecuting their own heretics, the Confucians and Taoists persecuting the Chinese Buddhists, or various sects of Japanese Buddhism persecuting each other. The entanglement of religion with politics is no solution to the contradiction of ethics versus the realities of power.

Again, Weber points out various efforts at consistency. The equivalent of an economic calling is a military calling, in which the religion makes a vocation out of war. This is the solution of Islam, and of the medieval Christian crusaders (and of certain fundamentalist Christians today). The other solution is again mystical withdrawal, radical pacifism of the sort found in Buddhism and some Hindu sects. But neither of these is a stable solution. The warfare religion is too unbrotherly, and tends eventually to a softening that brings ethics back in. Extreme religious pacifism is too unrealistic, and and can only exist where it is protected by a powerful state. (Even Buddhism, when it got state power in medieval Tibet, became militaristic.) Either way, the conflicts cannot be resolved.

What then is the "solution"? It is clear that Weber believes history has no solution. It is an endless set of tensions. Futhermore, he believes that these tensions grow worse in the modern era, for each area of modern life has grown more rationalized. The state has become bureaucractic. Religions are formulated for mass audiences and thought through by their own intellectuals. The economy of market capitalism imposes its own rational imperatives. Furthermore, the cultural life of modern people has become rationalized as well, by the rise of the medium of printing, widespread education, and other devices that universalize and intellectualize culture. Each sphere is increasingly rationalized, and increasingly independent of the others. Weber's view of the modern world is not of a single harmonious rationally—far from it! It is a set of different rationalized institutions, each following its own logic, and each in contradiction to the others. Modern culture, he asserts, is a search for solutions to these contradictions, although its solutions do not do away with the underlying problems. The intellectualization of life among the educated classes has resulted in elevating aesthetics into a kind of "salvation" in its own right. The enjoyment of art, literature, drama, or music becomes the most important thing to modern people. The arts provide a respite from the contradictions so manifest in the world of politics, the evident greed and lack of principle in economic life, and the inability of religion to provide a meaningful guidance amid these contradictions. But aesthetics merely privatizes the world into different "cults" worshiping their own subjective realities. Weber had in mind the concert-going museum-visiting, and book-reading audiences of his own day, but the model applies equally well to the cults of popular music, sports entertainment, and television drama that have become so dominant today.

Weber even anticipates a major theme of our modern private lives. He points out that the sexual sphere has always been a nonrationalized force in the world. Erotic passion cannot be calculated, and hence rationalized religions have always regarded it as an enemy. Monks and priests were supposed to be celibate, and sex became regarded as the worst temptation of the devil. In the modern world, though, as the power of the rationalized church has been challenged and cut down by the rivalry of other rationalized spheres of life, eroticism has come to have a new significance. We are weary of the rationalization of different life spheres, and the pressures to which they subject us. We need a respite from the impersonal realms of politics, economics, even from the contradictions of religion, the impersonality of science, and the irresolvable disputes of these different rationalized spheres against each other. Love is that respite. Precisely because it is irrational, it provides the personal element that the modern individual needs, to give some meaning to a world of conflicting institutions that have become too rational.

5

Weber's Vision of Social Change

One of the ironies of Max Weber's reputation is that some of his best books are among the least known. This is particularly so if one wants to get an overview, to find out what he really thought in a comprehensive way, about the actual processes of world history. Most of what he wrote was a specialized study on one aspect or another of society. Even though his studies of the religions of China and India and of ancient Judaism are quite lengthy, they are nevertheless applications of his method of ideal types, deliberately giving only a partial view of all the factors actually operative in social history. (As we shall see in the next chapter, however, his elaborate work on ancient Judaism encompasses quite a few dimensions.) *Economy and Society* is more comprehensive; it is not organized historically, however, but analytically around various topics, like the encyclopedia volume that it is. There are two main books in which Weber delineates his historical views, although these are among his least-known works: They are his *Agrarian Sociology of Civiizations,* which combines a lecture from his pre-breakdown years, 1896, and a volume on ancient Egypt, Mesopotamia, Greece, and Rome which he published in 1909; and *General Economic History,* which is the transcription of a course of lectures he gave in the last year of his life, 1919-1920.

Together, these give a comprehensive view of what Weber thought was the actual pattern of world history. It is not quite what one would expect, especially if one approaches Weber with the preconceived notion that he will give an idealist interpretation of history, stressing the independent power of religious ideas, or at least an overarching processing of rationalization. Instead we find a sociological analysis that emphasizes social institutions and material conditions. It is a view that is rather closer to Marx and Engels than to our stereotype derived from *The Protestant Ethic,* although it is a more complex and multidimensional picture of material and social conditions than the Marxian view offers. The material world is not only economic but geographical; social conflict and domination consist not only of class struggle but of military organization. Religion figures in the picture too, but less as free-floating ideas than as a set of organizations and interest groups in their own right, whose beliefs come out of a given political and social structure. Because these books are so little known, their ideas have not been fully developed in the sociological literature. There is an important theory, or set of theories, in *Agrarian Sociology* and *General Economic History* that remains waiting for us to put together. Weber himself makes his theoretical points in passing through the historical materials, rather than in sustained theoretical discussion. For those of us who want a truly powerful explanatory theory of historical change, these two books of Weber's remain a kind of buried treasure. (Only Marxist sociologist Perry Anderson (1974) has made use of Weber's *Agrarian Sociology*, which shows how close it is to an enriched materialist theory.)

In what follows I will sketch only some of the high points of these books. Weber is most famous for his theories of capitalism, so I will concentrate mainly on the full model contained in the last part of *General Economic History.* We will work backward, from the most developed form of rational capitalism to its preconditions, and through the links of a chain of prior causes. This same backward trajectory eventually brings us to *Agrarian Sociology*, which deals with the societies of the ancient Mediterranean. This is actually the topic that Weber knew the most about, because he began as a scholarly specialist in ancient Rome and its agricultural economy. Here I will briefly discuss Weber's theories of how geographical conditions affect both economic and military structures, and look over the nature of ancient capitalism, including its inner conflicts and its eventual downfall. There are other major bodies of ideas in these two books that I cannot address. For example, Weber has a very striking *political* theory of the family and sexual relationships, a theory of democracy, a theory of class conflict, and a theory of how religious ideas are shaped. The intellectual riches are overwhelming, and I can explore only some of the points of greatest interest. The analysis begins with his theory of the development of modern capitalism.

THE RISE OF RATIONAL CAPITALISM

Capitalism, says Weber (1961: 207-208, 260), is the provision of human needs by the method of enterprise, which is to say, by private businesses seeking profit. It is exchange carried out for positive gain, rather than forced contributions or traditionally fixed gifts or trades. Like all of Weber's categories, capitalism is an analytical concept; capitalism can be found as part of many historical economies, as far back as ancient Babylon. It became the indispensable form for the provision of everyday wants only in Western Europe around the middle of the nineteenth century. For this large-scale and economically predominant capitalism, the key is the "rational permanent enterprise" characterized by "rational capital accounting."

Weber himself used the term "rationalism" in a number of different senses. But for his *institutional* theory of capitalist development, there is only one sense that need concern us. The "rational capitalistic establishment," says Weber (1961: 207), "is one with capital accounting, that is, an establishment which determines its income yielding power by calculation according to the methods of modern bookkeeping and the striking of a balance." The key term is *calculability;* it occurs over and over again in those pages. What is distinctive about modern, large-scale, "rational" capitalism—in contrast to earlier, partial forms—is that it is methodical and predictable, reducing all areas of production and distribution as much as possible to a routine. This is also Weber's criterion for calling bureaucracy the most "rational" form of organization.

For a capitalist economy to have a high degree of predictability, it must have certain characteristics. The logic of Weber's argument is first to describe these characteristics; then to show the obstacles to them that were prevalent in virtually all societies of world history until recent centuries in the West; and, finally, by the method of comparative analysis, to show the social conditions responsible for their emergence.

According to his argument, the components of "rationalized" capitalism are as follows:

There must be *private appropriation of all the means of production,* and their concentration under the control of entrepreneurs. Land, buildings, machinery, and materials must all be assembled under a common management, so that decisions about their acquisition and use can be calculated with maximal efficiency. All these factors must be subject to sale as private goods on an open market. This development reaches its maximal scope when all such property rights are represented by commercial instruments, especially shares in ownership, which are themselves negotiable in a stock market.

Within this enterprise, capital accounting is optimized by a *technology that is "reduced to calculation to the largest possible degree"* (1961: 208). It is in this sense that mechanization is most significant for the organization of large-scale capitalism.

Labor must be free to move about to any work in response to conditions of demand. Weber notes that this is a formal and legal freedom, and that it goes along with the economic compulsion of workers to sell their labor on the market. Capitalism is impossible without a propertyless stratum selling its services "under the compulsion of the whip of hunger" (1961: 209), for only this completes a mass market system for the factors of production that makes it possible to clearly calculate the costs of products in advance.

Trading in the market must not be limited by irrational restrictions. That is to say, noneconomic restrictions on the movement of goods or of any of the factors of production must be minimized. Such restrictions include class monopolies upon particular items of consumption (such as sumptuary laws regulating dress), or upon ownership or work (such as prohibitions on townspeople owning land, or on knights or peasants carrying on trade; more extensively, caste systems in general). Other obstacles under this heading include transportation difficulties, warfare, and robbery—which make long distance trading hazardous and unreliable.

Finally, there must be *calculable law, both in adjudication and in public administration.* Laws must be couched in general terms applicable to all persons, and administered in such a way as to make the enforcement of economic contracts and rights highly predictable. Such a legal system is implicated in most of the above-cited characteristics of rational capitalism: the extension of private property rights over the factors of production; the subdivision and easy transferability of such rights through financial instruments and banking operations; formal freedom for laborers; and legally protected markets.

The picture that Weber gives us, then, is of the institutional foundations of the market as viewed by neoclassical economics. He sees the market as providing the maximal amount of calculability for the individual entrepreneur. Goods, labor, and capital flow continuously to the areas of maximal return; at the same time, competition in all markets reduces costs to their minimum. Thus prices serve to summarize all the necessary information about the optimal allocation of resources for maximizing profit; on this basis, entrepreneurs can most reliably make calculations for long-term production of large amounts of goods. "To sum up, " says Weber (1961: 209), "it must be possible to conduct the provision for needs exclusively on the basis of market opportunities and the calculation of net income."

It is, of course, the model of the laissez-faire capitalist economy that Weber wishes to ground. At the extreme, this is an unrealistic view of any economy that has ever existed. Weber treats it as an ideal type and, hence, in a fuller exposition would doubtless have been prepared to see it as only partially realized even in the great capitalist takeoff period of the nineteenth century. But it is worth noting that a critique of Weber along these lines could certainly not be a classical Marxian one. The central dynamic of capitalism in Marx's theory, in fact, depends even more immediately than Weber's on the unrestricted competitiveness of the open market for all factors of production. And Weber and Marx agree in claiming that the initial breakthrough to an industrial society had to occur in the form of capitalism. Thus, although Weber may have a personal bias toward the neoclassical market economy, both as analytical model and as political preference, this would give no grounds for a critique of the adequacy of his explanation of this phase of world history. Even for a later period, Weber is hardly dogmatic. As we shall see, he recognizes the possibility of socialism emerging, once capitalism has matured—although he does not admire the prospect—and he even gives some indications of the forces that might produce it. Like German and Austrian non-Marxist economists of his generation, Weber includes socialism within his analytical scheme.

Weber's model of the modern economy is particularly striking with regard to the concept of the "industrial revolution." For it is not mechanization per se that is the key to the economic transformation, despite the far-reaching consequences of shifts from agrarian to inanimate-energy-based technologies (see Lenski, 1966). In Weber's scheme, technology is essentially a dependent variable. The key *economic* characteristic of mechanization is that it is feasible only with mass production (Weber, 1961: 129, 247). The costs of even simpler machines such as steam-powered looms would make them worthless without a large-scale consumers' market for cloth, as well as a large-scale producers' market in wool or cotton. Similar considerations apply *a fortiori* to machinery on the scale of a steel rolling mill. But large-scale production is impossible without a high degree of predictability that markets will exist for the products, and that all the factors of production will be forthcoming at a reasonable cost. Thus mechanization depends on the prior emergence of all the institutional factors described above.

Weber does not elaborate a systematic theory of technological innovation, but it would be possible to construct one along these lines. He does note that all the crucial inventions of the period of industrial takeoff were the result of deliberate efforts to cheapen the costs of production (1961: 225-226, 231). These efforts took place because previous conditions had intensified the capitalist pursuit of profits. The same argument could be made, although Weber did not make it, in regard to the search for methods to improve agricultural production that took place in the seventeenth and eighteenth centuries. The "green revolution" that preceded (and made possible) the Industrial Revolution was not a process of mechanization (agricultural mechanization took place only in the late nineteenth century) but was, more simply, the application of capitalist methods of cost accounting to hitherto traditional agriculture. Thus it is the shift to the calculating practices of the capitalist market economy that makes technological innovation itself predictable, rather than, as previously, an accidental factor in economic life (1961: 231).

THE WEBERIAN CAUSAL CHAIN

What are the social preconditions for the emergence of capitalism as thus described?

Note, first of all, that economic life, even in the most prosperous of agrarian societies, generally lacked most of these traits. Property systems frequently tied land ownership to aristocratic status, and commercial occupations were often prohibited to certain groups and monopolized by others. The labor force was generally unfree—being either slaves or tied to the land as serfs. Technologies of mass production hardly existed. The market was generally limited either to local areas or to long-distance trade in luxuries, due to numerous near-confiscatory tax barriers, unreliable and varying coinage, warfare, robbery, and poor transportation. And legal systems, even in literate states, tended to be characterized by patrimonial or magical religious procedures, by differential application to different social groups and by different localities, and by the practices of officials seeking private gain. Reliable financial transactions, including the operation of a banking system relatively free from political interference and plundering, were particularly handicapped by these conditions.

The social preconditions for large-scale capitalism, then, involved the destruction of the obstacles to the free movement or economic transfer of labor, land, and goods. Other preconditions were the creation of the institutional supports for large-scale markets, especially the appropriate systems of property, law, and finance.

These are not the only preconditions of capitalism, but, specifically, Weber is seeking the organizational forms that made capitalism a world-transforming force in the West but not elsewhere. By a series of comparisons, Weber shows that a number of other factors that have been advanced to account for the Western takeoff cannot have been crucial. Against Sombart, he points out that standardized mass production for war cannot have been decisive, for although a good deal of this existed in Europe in the seventeenth century and thereafter, it also existed in the Mogul Empire and in China without giving an impetus to capitalism (1961: 229). Similarly, the enormous expenditures for court luxury found in both Orient and Occident were incapable of generating a mass market (1961: 229-230). Against the simpler arguments of Adam Smith, which attribute the industrial division of labor to the extension of trade, Weber points out that trade can be found everywhere, even in the Stone Age. In ancient Babylon, for example, trade was such as to disintegrate "primitive economic fixity" to a considerable degree (1961: 232). On the other hand, politically determined agrarian economies show how "specialization takes place without exchange" (1961: 103). Nor is the pursuit of profit per se the crucial motive for mass capitalism; the "ruthlessness" and "unscrupulousness" of the traditional foreign trader was incapable of transforming the economy at large (1961: 232). Nor can population growth have been the cause of Western capitalism, for the same trend occurred in China without the same result (1961: 258-259). Neither, finally, can the price revolution of the sixteenth century, due to the influx of precious metals from the Americas, have been decisive.

The features that Weber finds unique to the West constitute a causal chain, which is represented schematically in Figure 1. The characteristics of rational capitalism itself are the entrepreneurial organization of capital, rational technology, free labor, unrestricted markets, and calculable law. These make up a complex: The markers for goods, labor, and capital all mesh around entrepreneurial property using mass production technology; the operation of all of these factors together creates further pressures both to rationalize technology and to expand each factor market—yet distributing wealth in such a way as to further the demand. The legal system is both an ongoing prop for all of these features and a causal link backward to their social preconditions. At this intermediate causal level there is a second crucial factor that, like the law, is essentially cultural, although not in the sense of disembodied ideas, but, rather, in the sense of beliefs expressed in institutionalized behavior. This is the "lifting of the barrier . . . between internal and external ethics" (1961: 232).

In virtually all premodern societies there are two sharply divergent sets of ethical beliefs and practices. Within a social group, economic transactions are strictly controlled by rules of fairness, status, and tradition; in tribal societies, by ritualized exchanges with prescribed kin; in India, by rules of caste; in medieval Europe, by required contributions on the manor or to the great church properties. The prohibition on usury reflected this internal ethic, requiring an ethic of charity and the avoidance of calculation of gain from loans within the community. In regard to outsiders, however, economic ethics were at the opposite extreme: Cheating, price gouging, and loans at exorbitant interest were the rule. Both forms of ethic were obstacles to rational, large-scale capitalism: the internal ethic because it prevented the commercialization of economic life, the external ethic because it made trading relations too episodic and distrustful. The lifting of this barrier and the overcoming of this ethical dualism were crucial for the development of any extensive capitalism. Only this could make loans available regularly and promote the buying and selling of all services and commodities for moderate gain. Through innumerable daily repetitions, such small (but regular) profits could add up to much more massive economic transactions than could either the custom-bound or the predatory economic ethics of traditional societies.

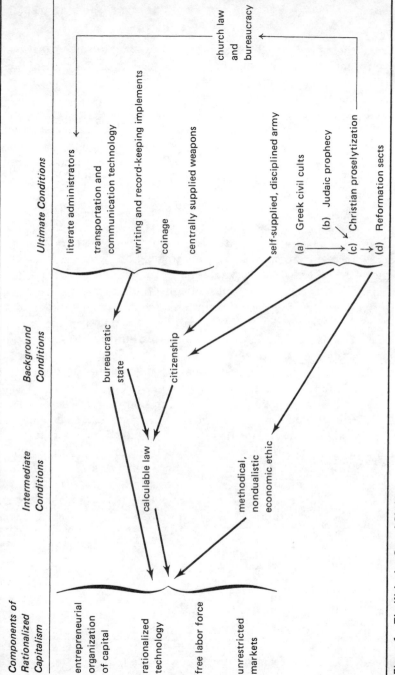

Figure 1. The Weberian Causal Chain

89

What, then, produced the calculable legal system of salable private property and free labor and the universal ethic of the pursuit of moderate economic profit? The next links in the causal chain are political and religious. The bureaucratic state is a crucial background determinant for all legal and institutional underpinnings of capitalism. Moreover, its legal system must be based on a concept of universal citizenship, which requires yet further political preconditions. The religious factor operates both as a direct influence on the creation of an economic ethic and as a final level of causality implicated in the rise of the rational-legal state and of legal citizenship.

The state is the factor most often overlooked in Weber's theory of capitalism. Yet it is the factor to which he gave the most attention; in *Economy and Society,* he devoted eight chapters of 680 pages to it, as opposed to one chapter of 235 pages to religion, with yet another chapter—the neglected but very important Chapter XV of Part II—to the relations between politics and religion. In the *General Economic History,* he gives the state the two penultimate chapters, religion the final chapter. For Weber, this political material was not an extraneous interest but, instead, the key to all of the *institutional* structures of rational capitalism. Only the West developed the highly bureaucratized state, based on specialized professional administrators and on a law made and applied by full-time professional jurists for a populace characterized by rights of citizenship. It is this bureaucratic-legal state that broke down feudalism and patrimonialism, freeing land and labor for the capitalist market. It is this state that pacified large territories, eliminated internal market barriers, standardized taxation and currencies. It is this state that provided the basis for a reliable system of banking, investment, property, and contracts, through a rationally calculable and universally applied system of law courts. One may even argue that the bureaucratic state was the proximate cause of the impulse to rationalization, generally—above all, via the late seventeenth- and eighteenth-century spirit of enlightened absolutism, which set the stage for the Industrial Revolution.

There are three causal questions about the rational/legal state. Why did it rise to predominance? Where did its structural characteristics come from? How did its legal system take the special form of conceiving of its subjects as holding the rights of citizenship?

The first question is easily answered. The bureaucratic state rose to predominance because it is the most efficient means of pacifying a large territory. It is effective externally in that it can supply a larger military, with better weapons, than can nonbureaucratic states; and it is effective, internally, as it tends to be relatively safe against disintegration by civil war or political *coup*.

The sources of the bureaucratic state are, to a degree, quite familiar. In the widely reprinted section on bureaucracy from *Economy and Society* (1968: 956-1005), Weber outlines the prerequisites: literate administrators, a technology of long-distance transportation and communication, writing and record-keeping materials, monetary coinage. The extent to which these could be put into effect, however, depended on a number of other factors. Geographical conditions such as easy transportation in river valleys, or favorable situations for state-controlled irrigation (1961: 237), fostered bureaucratic centralization, as did intense military competition among adjacent heartlands. Types of weapons that are centrally (rather than individually) supplied also favor bureaucratization. If such conditions make central control easy, however, bureaucratization need not proceed very deeply, and the society may be ruled by a thin stratum of officials above a local structure that remains patrimonial. In China, for example, this superficial bureaucratization constituted a long-term obstacle to capitalism, as it froze the economy under the patrimonial control of local clans.

The most thorough bureaucratization, as well as that uniquely favorable to capitalism, is that which incorporates a formalistic legal code based on citizenship. Citizenship meant, first of all, membership in a city; by extension, membership in a state and hence holding political rights within it. This was an alien concept throughout most of history. In the patrimonial state, political office was a form of private property or personal delegation, and even in most premodern quasi-bureaucratic states the populace at large was only subject to the state, not the holder of rights within it. The latter condition arose only in the West. In both Mediterranean antiquity and the European Middle Ages, cities came under the control of brotherhoods of warriors banded together for mutual protection. Such cities had their own laws and courts, administered by the citizens themselves, all of whom stood under it in relation of formal equality. Such citizenship rights remained historically significant after the original civic forms changed or disappeared. The formal rights and legal procedures originally applied only to a local elite, but when cities were incorporated into large-scale bureaucratic states, they provided the basis for a much more widely inclusive system of adjudication. This was the case when Rome, originally one of these military-fraternity cities, became an empire and, again, in the Middle

Ages, when cities in alliance with kings lost their independence but contributed their legal structures to the larger states.

Nearing the end of our chain of causality, we ask: What factors enabled this distinctive type of city to arise in the West? Weber gives two conditions: one military, the other religious.

The military condition is that in the West the city consisted of "an organization of those economically competent to bear arms, to equip and train themselves" (1961: 237). This was the case in the formative period of the ancient Greek and Italian cities and, again, in the medieval cities with their disciplined infantries fielded by the guilds. In both cases, the money power of the cities bolstered their military power and, hence, democratization and concomitant legal citizenship. In the Orient and in ancient Egypt, on the contrary, the military princes with their armies were older than the cities and, hence, legally independent cities did not arise; Weber attributed this pattern to the impetus to early centralization given by the irrigation.

The second condition is that in the East, magical taboos prevented the organization of military alliances among strangers and, hence, did not allow formation of independent cities. In India, for example, the ritual exclusion of castes had this effect. More generally, in Asia and the Middle East, the traditional priests held monopolies over communion with the gods, whereas in Western antiquity it was the officials of the city who themselves performed the rites (1961: 238). In the one case, the boundaries of religious communion reinforced preexisting group divisions; in the other, religious boundaries were an explicit political tool by which civic alliances could be established and enlarged. It is at this point that the two main lines of Weber's chain of causality converge.

We have been tracing the causal links behind the emergence of the rational/legal state, which is one of the two great intermediate conditions of the emergence of an open market economy. The other great intermediate condition (noted earlier) is an economic ethic that breaks the barrier between internal and external economies. Now we see that the religious factors that produced the citizenship revolution and those that produced the economic ethic are essentially the same.

Our last question, then, is this: What brought about this religious transformation? Weber gives a series of reasons, each intensifying the effects of the last (1961: 238). Ethical prophecy within ancient Judaism was important, even though it did not break down ritual barriers between Jews and Gentiles, because it established a tradition of hostility to magic, the main ethos within which barriers flourished. The transformation of Christianity from a Jewish sect into a proselytizing universal religion gave this tradition widespread currency, while the pentacostal spirit of Christian proselytization set aside the ritual barriers among clans and tribes, which still characterized the ancient Hellenistic cities to some degree. The Judeo-Christian innovations are not the whole story, however; the earlier development of Greek religion into the civic cults had already done much to make universalistic legal membership possible.

The religious factors, as we have seen, entwine with political ones, and their influence in the direction of legal citizenship and upon an economic ethic have fluctuated historically. There is no steady or inevitable trend toward increasing rationalization of these spheres, but Western history does contain a series of episodes that happen to have built up these effects at particular points in time, so that eventually a whole new economic dynamic was unleashed. On the political side, the Christian cities of the Middle Ages, drawing upon the institutional legacies of the ancient world, were able to establish religiously sworn confraternities that reestablished a legal system based on citizenship. A second political factor was fostered by religion: The Christian church provided the literate administrators, the educational system, and the example of its own bureaucratic organization as bases upon which the bureaucratic states of the West could emerge. And, on the strictly motivational side, the development of European Christianity gave a decisive ethical push toward rationalized capitalism.

Here, at last, we seem to touch base with Weber's original Protestant Ethic thesis. But in the mature Weber, the thesis is greatly transformed. Protestantism is only the last intensification of one of the chains of factors leading to rational capitalism. Moreover, its effect now is conceived to be largely negative, in the sense that it removes one of the last institutional obstacles diverting the motivational impetus of Christianity away from economic rationalization. For, in medieval Christianity, the methodical, disciplined organization of life was epitomized by the monastic communities. Although the monasteries contributed to economic development by rationalizing agriculture and promoting their own industries, Weber generally saw them as obstacles to the full capitalist development of the secular economy. As long as the strongest religious motivation was siphoned off for essentially otherworldly ends, capitalism in general could not take off (1961: 267-269). Hence the Reformation was most significant because it abolished the monasteries. The most advanced section of the economy would, henceforth, be secular. Moreover, the highest ethics of a religious life could no longer be confined to monks but had to apply to ordinary citizens living in the world. Calvinism and the other voluntary sects were the most intense version of this motivation, not because of the idea of predestination (which no longer receives any mention in Weber's last text) but only because they required a specific religious calling for admission into their ranks, rather than automatic and compulsory membership in the politically more conservative churches. Weber's (1961: 269-270) last word on the subject of Protestantism was simply this:

> The development of the concept of the calling quickly gave to the modern entrepreneur a fabulously clear conscience—and also industrious workers; he gave to his employees as the wages of their ascetic devotion to the calling and of co-operation in his ruthless exploitation of them through capitalism the prospect of eternal salvation, which in an age when ecclesiastical discipline took control of the whole of life to an extent inconceivable to us now, represented a reality quite different from any it has today. The Catholic and Lutheran churches also recognized and practiced ecclesiastical discipline. But in the Protestant ascetic communities admission to the Lord's Supper was conditioned on ethical fitness, which again was identified with business honor, while into the content of one's faith no one inquired. Such a powerful, unconsciously refined organization for the production of capitalistic individuals has never existed in any other church or religion.

WEBER'S GENERAL THEORY OF HISTORY

Is there an overall pattern in Weber's argument? It is not a picture of a linear trend toward ever-increasing rationality. Nor is it an evolutionary model of natural selection, in the sense of random selection of the more advanced forms, accumulating through a series of stages. For Weber's constant theme is that the *pattern of relations among the various factors* is crucial in determining their effect upon economic rationalization. Any one factor occurring by itself tends to have opposite effects, overall, to those it has in combination with the other factors.

For example, self-supplied military coalitions produce civic organizations and legal systems that are favorable to capitalism. But if the self-armed civic groups are too strong, the result is a series of guild monopolies that stifle capitalism by overcontrolling markets. Cities, on the other hand, have to be balanced by the bureaucratic state. But when the state is too strong by itself, it, too, tends to stifle capitalism. This can happen by bolstering the immobility of labor (as in the case of "the second serfdom" produced in Russia and eastern Europe as absolutist states developed in the seventeenth and eighteenth centuries); or by directly controlling the division of labor by forced contributions instead of allowing a market to develop. In the areas of the world where bureaucratization was relatively easy, as in ancient Egypt or China, or the Byzantine Empire, the unrestrained power of the state stereotyped economic life and did not allow the dynamics of capitalism to unfold.

The same is true of the religious variables. The creation of the great world religions, with their universalism and their specialized priesthoods, was crucial for the possibility of breaking the ritual barriers among localized groups, with all the consequences this might have for subsequent developments. But, in the absence of other factors, this could actually bolster the obstacles to capitalism. This happened in India, where the development of Hinduism fostered the castle system; the universalistic religion set an external seal upon the lineup of particularistic groups that happened to exist at the time. Even in Christianity, where moral prophecy had a much more barrier-breaking and world-transforming effect, the Church (in the period when it was predominant) created another obstacle against its capitalist implications. This was the period of the High Middle Ages in Europe, when monasticism proliferated and thus channeled all the energy of religious motivation into a specialized role and away from the economic concerns of ordinary life.

Weber saw the rise of large-scale capitalism, then, as the result of a series of combinations of conditions that had to occur together. This makes world history look like the result of configurations of events so rare as to appear accidental. Weber's position might well be characterized as historicist, in the sense of seeing history as a concatenation of unique events and unrepeatable complexities. Once a crucial conjuncture occurs, its results transform everything else—and not just locally but also in the larger world of competing states. This was true of the great charismatic revelations of the world religions, which shut off China, India or the West from alternative lines of development as well as determined the ways that states upon these territories would interact with the rest of the world. Similarly, the full-scale capitalist breakthrough itself was a once-only event, radiating outward to transform all other institutions and societies. Hence the original conditions necessary for the emergence of capitalism were not necessary for its continuation. The original religious ethic could fade, once the calculability of massive economic transactions had become a matter of routine. Hence late-industrializing states need not follow the route of classic capitalism. In the advanced societies, the skeleton of the economic structure might even be taken over by socialism.

Weber's account of the rise of capitalism, then, is in a sense not a theory at all, in that it is not a set of universal generalizations about economic change. Nevertheless, on a more abstract level, Weber is at least implicitly proposing such a theory. On one level, his work may be read as a collection of separate hypotheses about specific processes and their effects. The foregoing caveat about the necessary balance among factors may be incorporated by specifying that the causal variables must operate at a given strength—that is, by turning them into quantitative generalizations specified to a given range of variation.

On a second level, one may say that the fundamental generalizations in Weber's theory of capitalism concern the crucial role of balances and tensions between opposing elements. "All in all," says Weber in a little-known passage (1968: 1192-1193), "the specific roots of Occidental culture must be sought in the tension and peculiar balance, on the one hand, between office charisma and monasticism, and on the other between the contractual character of the feudal state and the auton-omous bureaucratic hierocracy." In other words, the main features of the West depend on a tension between the routinization of religious charisma in the church and the participatory communities of monks, and on a tension between the democratizing tendencies of self-supplied armies and the centralized bureaucratic state. These give us Weber's two great intermediate factors, a nondualistic religious ethic and calculable law, respectively. No one element must predominate if rationalization is to increase. More concretely, because each "element" is composed of real people struggling for precedence, the creation of a calculable, open-market economy depends upon a continuous balance of power among differently organized groups. The formal egalitarianism of the law depends upon balances among competing citizens and among competing jurisdictions. The nondualistic economic ethic of moderated avarice depends upon a compromise between the claims of in-group charity and the vicious circle of out-group rapaciousness.

The capitalist economy depends on this balance. The open-market system is a situation of institutionalized strife. Its essence is struggle, in an expanded version of the Marxian sense, but with the qualification that this could go on continuously, and indeed must, if the system is to survive. Hence if there is any generalization implicit in Weber's theory applicable to economic history after the initial rise of capitalism, it is this: The possibility for the follower-societies of the non-Western world to acquire the dynamism of industrial capitalism depends on there being a balance among class forces, and among competing political forces and cultural forces as well. In the highly industrialized societies, also, the continuation of capitalism depends on continuation of the same conflicts. The victory of any one side would spell the doom of the system. In this respect, as in others, Weber's theory is a conflict theory indeed.

WEBER'S AGRARIAN SOCIOLOGY: MATERIAL CONDITIONS AND SOCIAL STRUCTURE

Weber's *Agrarian Sociology of Ancient Civilizations* (1909/1976) takes us back to the era in which the most remote preconditions he discusses in *General Economic History* were formed. Here he is not concerned primarily with tracing the development of this particular form of capitalism, but with describing the development of these ancient societies in their own right. The *Agrarian Sociology* in this sense is the more general of the two books, at least in its theoretical outlook, if not in the number of societies upon which it draws. Weber gives a multi-dimensional explanation of why Egypt, Babylon and other Mesopotamian societies, Greece, and Rome had their distinctive social patterns. But certain major factors stand out; it was their combination that caused each of these societies (and various historical epochs for each of them) to have its own "historical individuality."

An important background factor in every case is geographical. Egypt and Mesopotamia developed as river valley civilizations. Their economies were based on irrigation, hence as centralized and rather bureaucratic organization from the very outset. But a further geographical factor made Egypt and Mesopotamia diverge. Egypt was dominated from early on by the great temples and their priests, and the kingship when it arose was always closely linked to this bureaucratic temple economy, as a kind of theocracy. Mesopotamia, on the other hand, was more often split among rival city-states, fighting to establish empires over one another. Hence the Mesopotamian kings became independent and superior to the temple priests, though they continued their bureaucratic control. The difference between Egypt and Mesopotamia in this respect was that Egypt was geographically isolated, surrounded by deserts and hence relatively inaccessible to military conquerors. Mesopotamia, however, was the land of two great rivers (the Tigris and the Euphrates), and was surrounded by lands that supported nomad populations who periodically constituted a military threat. Military kings soon became more important than the temples. For this reason, Egypt was always the most bureaucratic, centrally controlled, and socially conservative part of the ancient world. Mesopotamia was more dynamic, with its rise and fall of military states, and its innovations in religion following changes of power. Mesopotamia, too, had more economic dynamism. Whereas in Egypt virtually all production and distribution was managed bureaucratically by the state (and hence could dispense with the use of money), in Babylon a form of capitalist trade emerged. Money, banking, and a legal system regarding loans and debts were developed.

In the years when all this was developing (from approximately 3000 B.C. to after 1000 B.C.), Greece was a remote and barbaric fringe. Early Greek social organization consisted of coalitions of tribes, held together by provisional religious cults and by the sheer military fortunes of the group. The early Greek settlements were fortresses along the coast, where petty "kings" carried out a combination of piracy and trade. The state always has a military core, Weber points out, but economic factors enter into it too. These kings were able to build their power because they monopolized foreign trade (which in those days was feasible only by ship, land transport being extremely difficult). Eventually some of the Greek citadels went from being the passive hosts of Middle Eastern merchants to active trading expeditions, and even to overseas colonization. Along with this expansion of the Greek economy came a change in military technology that overturned the early kings. The relatively expensive bronze weapons that were the basis for an aristocratic monopoly upon violence gave way to cheaper iron weapons. The Greek peasants around the cities became organized into efficient armies, and democratization set in. Through a series of revolutions, the citadel kingdoms turned into a variety of citizen-controlled city states.

Implicitly there was also a geographical factor in this development. Let us ask why Greece did not turn into a large centralized kingdom of the sort found in the Middle East. The reason is that Greece is a complex of mountainous peninsulas and islands, with little pockets of good farming land making up population centers here and there. Transport was mainly by sea, but this served primarily to distribute the Greeks into different parts of the Mediterranean (including especially the coast of Asia Minor, as well as southern Italy and Sicily), rather than consolidating power. It is true that later on centralized states developed, beginning with Alexander the Great (around 300 B.C.), and then on a much larger scale with the Roman empire. But these took a long time to build, and in the meantime the pattern of ancient Greek civilization was established.

Rome in its earlier development was quite parallel to Greece: the coalition of tribes under a religious cult, the aristocratic kingship, the coming of the mass peasant armies, and the pressures toward democratization. But Rome differed in several crucial respects. For one thing, Italy had much larger stretches of fertile land, and could build larger populations within the same political unit. Rome was located in just such a fertile plain. Furthermore, it was not as protected by natural barriers as the Greek cities, and had to adopt a stance of full and continuous military mobilization against its neighbors. Rome was also the trade center of the peninsula, and hence early amassed the wealth that enabled it to support a large army. Once Rome had conquered its nearby enemies, it had a territorial and population base that made it a military power on a scale until then unheard of in Greece. With further conquests, this advantage grew steadily larger, and eventually Rome established an empire around the entire Mediterranean. (It included Egypt, but not Mesopotamia; and it expanded west and north to what are now France, Britain, and much of Germany and the Balkans.)

As Rome expanded as a military state, its economy shifted. From a society of peasant farmers who were called periodically to war, it became divided into a professional army, an urban population of the very rich and the very poor, and a slave sector working on plantations. Parts of this development had already happened in the Greek city-states; though they never shifted from the citizen army to mercenaries (that is, before the Roman conquest demilitarized them), they too had shifted to a slave-based economy. This was one of the distinctive characteristics of their civilizations in what we call the "classical" period.

THE NATURE OF ANCIENT CAPITALISM

Was the ancient world capitalist? Weber addressed himself explicitly to this issue. The question becomes an important one once we rid ourselves of a certain mode of evolutionary thinking. We are used to believing that the ancient Mediterranean societies were a kind of earlier stage in our history. In the most simpleminded formulation, the sequence goes: primitive tribal societies, then ancient, medieval, and modern. Marx and Engels used this kind of model too; because they were economic determinists, each type of society was an economic stage, thus running: primitive communism, slave economy, feudalism, capitalism. Weber rejects this kind of stage model. The breakthrough to "civilization" happened several thousand years ago with the development of a high level of agricultural production and the use of iron tools and weapons, which could support cities, a literate middle and upper class, and the great philosophical "world religions." In modern terminology, Egypt, Babylon, ancient Greece, Rome, and medieval Europe—also medieval China, India, and the Islamic world—were all "agrarian" societies, possessing large populations and a complex stratification based upon the extraction of surplus. They are all on the same level. Slavery and feudalism are not different stages; they are merely different variants in what was technologically and ecologically the same basic type of society.

Hence the question of capitalism should be asked in a different light. The ancient societies were not a stage on the way to medieval societies, which in turn were an inevitable step before modern capitalism. Weber totally rejected this way of looking at history. Instead, the appropriate question to ask is, Why didn't the ancient Mediterranean societies develop capitalism? And Weber's answer is: They did. But capitalism comes in several varieties, and the form they developed was not the type he called "rational" or "modern" capitalism. But Weber was not chauvinistic about the use of the word. He explicitly says (1909/1976: 48-51) that ancient society had its own form of capitalism. Its dynamics can be investigated, and the reasons it went in a different direction from the capitalism of modern society can be discovered.

Actually, one should say that Weber describes several forms of ancient capitalism. We recall that "modern" capitalism depends on the movement of all factors of production and consumption upon the market, and that is what gives it its peculiarly "rational" character. Among other factors of production is human labor. Weber regards the labor market as most "rational" when laborers are free, capable of moving in response to the supply and demand of the market. Ancient societies had this to only a small degree. The predominant form of labor in classical Greece and Rome was slavery. But this should not be regarded as absolutely uncapitalistic. You could just as well say it is even more capitalistic, in the sense that labor itself is made into a commodity that is bought and sold.

In addition, there are the ways in which slaves are procured. In earlier Greek society, people became slaves mainly because they went into debt, and eventually lost their freedom when they could not pay off. This already implies another aspect of capitalism: namely, a system of credit, so that loans and debts can exist. In fact, Weber characterizes the major class divisions of ancient society as those between debtors and creditors, classes on a credit market. It was this that made up the major class conflicts of the time, rather than a class conflict between slaves and slave owners (which Marx and Engels thought was the main class conflict). Weber points out that the politics of the ancient city-states always centered on a struggle between the debt-ridden lower classes of freemen and the wealthy land-owning and money-lending aristocracy. It was these two groups that made up the democrats and the conservatives, the plebians and the patricians, who are the historical actors of the classical period. The tradition of democracy, which we in the modern world have inherited from ancient Greece, was due to the fact that the democratic faction won, at least part of the time. They forced the enlargement of the franchise, and they caused some periodic reforms that mitigated their debts and restricted the power of wealthy creditors. Weber argues that military factors were mainly responsible for this democratization. The Greek cities needed as many troops as possible for their citizen-armies, hence they had to make concessions to the democratic side, lest their soldiers disappear into debt-slavery. Rome, on the other hand, did not go so far in the direction of democratization, although these classes fought their own civil wars and made some concessions to mass citizenship. The wealth brought by its military conquests made possible a different route, which included the shift to paid mercenary soldiers, eventually undermining what democracy had been attained. In both cases, this is class conflict, shaped around interest groups on a market: the class conflicts of a particular kind of capitalism.

The other way in which slaves could be acquired was by purchase. This was even more capitalist in nature, because it required that there be a slave market. Where did these slaves come from? Not from debt-slavery, because part of the Greek democratic reforms was to prohibit selling citizens into slavery for their debts. Instead, slaves were brought from abroad. Part of this was the result of warfare. When the Greeks and Romans conquered a foreign people (or just went on a slave-hunting raid), they could sell their victims into slavery. As these dominant societies became richer, moreover, the peripheral societies around them (especially in the Black Sea, the area of what is now southern Russia and Turkey) came to enslave their own even more remote neighbors, bringing them to the slave markets of Greece and Rome. In this way a full-blown slave-market developed, with its prices rising and falling in response to supply and demand. It was, in short, a distinctive form of capitalism that we can call slave-capitalism.

Slaves were thus used for agricultural production, for working in mines, and for handicrafts and industry. Slaves were allowed to buy their freedom, so they could even set themselves up in their own businesses, to purchase their liberty. The Greek economy came to depend to a large degree on the work of slaves, even in the skilled trades and in banking. Slave overseers managed other slaves. This development was carried especially far in Rome. Because it was a far wealthier society than Greece, Rome came to be dominated economically by huge plantations worked by thousands of slaves and owned by the Roman aristocracy.

This account is oversimplified in various respects. There were other forms of economy coexisting with slave capitalism. There were still some independent free peasants. There were also some free merchants engaging in merchant capitalism. Temples were economic units too, and they engaged in banking as well as their own production (especially of wine and olive oil, the main cash crops) for the market. There was a market for land, fed especially by the conquered territories that became available for sale through Roman conquest; though the peasant-army lobbied for the distribution of land to themselves, the wealthy aristocrats were usually able to rent it to themselves to exploit for profit. Weber refers to this last style of enterprise as "colonial booty capitalism"; this kind of enterprise went hand in hand with a form of political capitalism that consisted of buying the rights to collect taxes.

Together, these various forms of capitalism brought about a dynamic takeoff of the ancient economy. The Greek cities, especially Rome, expanded production and became a wealthy civilization, creating the urban monuments that are still visible today. But ancient capitalism contained the seeds of its own downfall. For one thing, the industrial sector was somewhat stagnant. Because the work was done by slaves, there was little incentive to expand production. Furthermore, the whole basis of the slave economy depended upon military expansion. When the Roman empire stopped growing, the supply of slaves began to dry up. The central market of the economy began to go out of existence.

One response was to try to breed more slaves, but this undermined the more centralized economic units of the time. In the large slave-worked plantations and mines, slaves generally were kept in barracks, living without families. Increasing the slave population meant the slaves had to be reorganized, allowed to marry and to settle in households of their own. The slaves began to be transformed into peasants on the rural estates, not free peasants but tied to the land. In short, they became serfs, and ancient slave society became feudalism. This shift toward a rural society of serfdom was paralleled from another direction. The old free population of the Mediterranean cities had been reduced to poverty by the wealthy classes who monopolized the landed economy; eventually they began to place themselves under the protection of aristocratic patrons, who assigned them little plots on their country estates. The free population sank into serfdom, meeting the slave population that was rising to the same point.

With this crisis and transformation of the slave economy into rural subsistence, the monetary economy began to fade. This made it increasingly difficult for the Roman state to collect taxes. It began to impose a system of forced contributions; citizens paid not money but a certain amount of food or goods to the imperial storehouses, or donated labor (from their slaves and serfs) for the state roads and construction projects. This too made a vicious circle. The more the state depended on these kinds of nonmonetary contributions, the more it encouraged a local subsistence-level economy. Markets faded away. Eventually the military basis of the Roman state had to change, as mercenary soldiers could no longer be paid or even well supplied from the central storehouses. Instead, soldiers had to be settled on the land, which gave them a kind of feudal independence from central authority. The Roman army that fell victim to the German invaders in the late 300s and 400s A.D. was no longer constituted by the disciplined peasant citizens who had won the empire, or even the professional mercenaries who had replaced them at the height of the Roman slave economy. Rome did not fall from outside conquest, Weber concluded; it had already transformed itself into a feudal society from within.

Weber ended his analysis of ancient economies by comparing them to that of the European Middle Ages. The feudalism of the south he regarded as stagnant; it was the failure of a monetary economy, the graveyard of ancient slave capitalism. In the north and northeast of Europe, however, geographical conditions were fostering yet another social form. Just as the geography of the ancient Near East and Mediterranean had shaped the basic social forms of the river-valley civilizations and the coastal city-states, the different ecology of the North would shape civilization in another direction. Northern civilization was to be land based where transportation was feeble, and hence military centralization was long in coming. Moreover, medieval Europe was a land of pioneers, of small groups working their way into the forests, slowly clearing plots of land and settling upon them. It was this ecology that produced the small farm, and the distinctive individualism of private property. Eventually when larger state units were formed, it happened slowly and by incorporating much of this decentralization and individualism into them. Medieval cities emerged on a different basis than the ancient city-states. Here we tie up with the story of the emergence of modern capitalism, which Weber treated in *General Economic History*.

6

The Comparative Studies of the World Religions

During World War I, Weber published three studies of world religions. In their English translations they are known as *The Religion of China* (1916/1951) (Confucianism and Taoism), *The Religion of India* (1916-17/1958c) (Hinduism and Buddhism), and *Ancient Judaism* (1917-1919/1952). There were to be three more studies, on early Christianity, medieval Christianity, and Islam. Weber did not live to write these. Altogether the six studies would have covered the philosophical religions of the great world civilizations. They would have surveyed the range of answers that religious intellectuals have given to the meaning of existence, and they would have shown how these different religious worldviews have affected the development of their societies.

Weber was pursuing his theme of *The Protestant Ethic* on a much grander scale. *The Protestant Ethic* turns out to have been a preliminary study. The larger project was to show how all kinds of religious ideas had effects upon economic action, in short, to answer the question of why modern capitalism broke through in Western Europe rather than in China, India, or elsewhere on the globe. But even considering its huge size, Weber's comparative religious study was still restricted. It was intended to show the effects of one factor, religious ideas, upon economic development. As we have seen, Weber recognized other factors as well, especially institutional ones. Because these are entwined with religious organization in various ways (see Figure 1 in Chapter 5), he cannot avoid dealing with these aspects in his comparative religion volumes, but that is not their main focus. After finishing the six studies of religions he planned to write a master work that would bring together all the factors, combining religion with other institutions and historical conditions that would finally answer the question of the origins of Western capitalism.

Weber died before he came close to finishing his ambitious plan. But, as we have seen in the previous chapter, he did leave a sketch of what the overall product would have looked like. He would have had finally to resolve the conflict between the two sides of his personality, and decide how to weigh ideal and material factors in relation to each other. In *General Economic History* and *Agrarian Sociology*, he gave prominence to the material factors, though he saw them in a complex way. In the comparative religious studies, generally he tried to stress the autonomous effects of ideas. But even here he had a tendency to delve into the material conditions, especially political ones. One can even extract from these works (along with other parts of his writings) a theory of how organizational and political conditions actually influence the development and adoption of religious ideas. There is a sociology of religion contained in these works that makes religion an effect of social conditions and not just a cause. Conceivably the strain of admitting this contradiction in his worldviews contributed to Weber's death before he could finish his life work.

ANCIENT JUDAISM

The third of Weber's comparative religious studies was on *Ancient Judaism* (1917-1919/1952). But I will treat it first here. It is the most central of all his studies to the theme of the emergence of Western capitalism, given that Judaism is the origin of the religious conceptions that eventually became Christianity. As Weber's overall scheme shapes up, Christianity in general rather than Protestantism is the main driving force behind rational capitalism. Thus we will see where this world-transforming religion came from, and then compare the conditions in the Orient that sent its religions, and hence its social structures, in a different direction.

The social organization of the people of ancient Palestine at first resembled that of Greece. Geography had something to do with this, Weber pointed out. Palestine was an area suitable for small farmers and wandering herdsmen, and was in between the two great river-valley civilizations in Egypt and Mesopotamia. Though always in danger of foreign conquest, its indigenous structure was decentralized rather than bureaucratically authoritarian like its neighbors. Small cities grew along the trade routes. The kinship group was the basic form of social organization, a kind of coalition of families for mutual help and defense; and these in turn were organized into larger coalitions, the tribes. What eventually became Israel emerged as a coalition of ten such tribes.

Weber describes this society as undergoing a class conflict similar to that occuring in Greece. As long as the kinship groups were wanderers with primitive weapons, there was a rough equality at least among adult males, and only a certain prestige granted to their leaders or patriarchs (such as Abraham). But as the population began to settle on the land, as well as to establish cities, social classes appeared. Just as in Greece, a wealthier aristocracy developed that monopolized the trade in the cities, and forced the peasant farmers into their debt. This was exacerbated by a change in weaponry. The advent of expensive horse-drawn chariots and armor tended to make fighting the monopoly of the wealthy upper class. The small farmers were in danger of becoming debt-slaves, like the corresponding class in Greece.

Just as in Greece, a class struggle went on between these two groups. As in Greece, the lower classes in Palestine won important victories. Here again the guiding force was military. For at the same time that the cities and their aristocracies were beginning to develop, the tribes had formed a kind of super-alliance for action against their neighbors: the Yahwe Confederacy. Yahwe was the Hebrew name, translated in the English Bible as Jehovah, of the war god whose worship held the Confederacy together. Yahwe was not the only god recognized at the time; there were also the gods of the enemy peoples—Baal, Moloch, and so forth, who later were degraded to the status of devils. Also, the separate tribes and kin-groups within the Confederacy at first had their own family gods and spirits. The Yahwe Confederacy was a central feature of Palestine politics, and as it grew more powerful, it became increasingly monotheistic. It attacked the rival religious cults, declared them to be false worshipers, and monopolized religious worship for its own god.

The Yahwe Confederacy played an important part in the class warfare of the time. It was basically a rural cult, and it upheld the old tribal equality of all people (or rather, all adult males) against the city aristocracy. It formulated a code of ethics that called for charity to one's tribal brothers, in opposition to the loans and foreclosures of the city elites. The forgiveness of debts (a formula taken over in the Christian Lord's Prayer) comes from this originally political program. It attacked the morality of the cities, which it saw as hotbeds of debauchery and sin (hence the story of Sodom and Gomorah). It formulated strict rules of sexual morality, in opposition to the fertility rituals, with their sexual orgiasticism and temple prostitution, which were characteristic of some of the city religions. Various taboos distinctive to Judaism, such as not eating pork or meat with blood on it, were the result of an effort to dissociate its people from the sacrificial religions of its rivals.

Most important, Yahwe was regarded as an all-powerful god who granted victory in battle. The prestige of the Confederacy and its god was boosted to a very high level when David defeated the Philistines (that is, the Phoenicians, the city dwellers of the Mediterranean coast) and established the first unified kingdom in Palestine. But the underlying political conflicts did not go away. David's successors, especially Solomon, began to deviate from the pure rural morality of the Confederacy and to imitate the splendor of the Egyptian and Mesopotamian kings. The hated city classes and the non-Yahweist cults continued to thrive, while the peasants were excluded from the now-professional, chariot-driving army, and were oppressed by debt. It is likely that the memory of the Yahwe Confederacy would eventually have faded in a few generations, and the kingdom of Jerusalem would have become just another Mesopotamian-style state, but political circumstances intervened.

For Palestine was in between the two great empires of the time, the Egyptian and the Assyrian, and as a small state it did not really stand a chance of surviving long as independent. The power of Jerusalem weakened as the Assyrian armies expanded on the far horizon. In this circumstance arose the distinctive Jewish religious innovation: the prophets. The tradition the prophets were drawing upon goes back to inspired warriors in the old coalition, men who went into a frenzy as battle approached, and whose words and deeds were regarded as divinely inspired. This type of religious battle frenzy was known in many warrior societies (among the Vikings, for example, they were called berserkers, from which comes our word "berserk"). But the situation in Palestine gave them a special twist. For the old peasant armies had been demilitarized, their armies replaced by the professional army of the city. Memories remained of the old Yahwe Confederacy and the victories it had won, however, and the old tradition of ecstatic warriors reappeared in the guise of unarmed prophets, holy men who wandered in the desert and the countryside, and who came to the cities to interpret the inspiration Yahwe had given them.

Their message was one of denunciation. Speaking for the rural populace, they accused the kings of sinning against the laws of Yahwe. This was an astounding thing for them to do, compared to religious leaders of other societies. In Mesopotamia or Egypt, religious speakers never had this kind of independence; their oracles always had to speak for the king, never against him. In Greece, too, oracles were under the power of the secular cities, and could not raise this kind of moral objection to public policy. But in Palestine the political situation gave the representatives of the old rural war-Confederacy the freedom to speak against the kings of the cities, precisely because these city kings had not really consolidated their power over the residents of the countryside. Furthermore, their power in the international arena was weak and everyone knew it. Most of Palestine was soon gobbled up by the advancing Assyrian empire. The prophets interpreted this, not as a failure of their god (which is what usually happened in the religious politics of other defeated states) but as Yahwe's punishment upon the people of Israel for having broken the covenant. The prophecy had come true. The prophets ventured another: When Israel returned to the conditions of righteousness, Yahwe would restore them to political power.

Again history intervened. For if the Assyrian power had remained in place, Israel and its religious beliefs would have been doomed eventually. But a century later, when memory of the prophecies was still alive, the Assyrians were overthrown by the Babylonians. Many of the Jews were carried into exile, the largest portion of them going to Babylon itself, where they became an urban, merchant people rather than a rural population. (Other Jews, however, went to Egypt and elsewhere in the Middle East, where they later provided the population base within which Christianity originally spread.) In Babylon, the Jews tried to remain faithful to their own religion. The taboos and rituals against participating in foreign cults were drawn more sharply. This preserved a separate Jewish identity, and has been important in keeping the Jews as a distinctive group for over two thousand years since.

It was at this point, Weber argued, that the distinctive Judaic religious ethic was crystalized, which was to have such an important effect upon Western history. Yahwe had originally been a purely worldly god, bringing victory in war. But as Israel became demilitarized, the religion had to either disappear, along with other failed military cults, or change into a religion that exalted inner, moral conditions rather than external ones. Righteousness became important rather than the enthusiasm of warriors in battle. Religious motivations were harnessed to personal self-control. But since the Jews expected that eventually their worldly kingdom would be restored, their activity did not go in a purely mystical, other-worldly direction. It laid the basis for the "inner-worldly asceticism" that Weber regarded as its distinctive contribution to the eventual rise of capitalism. Furthermore, the tendency of other religions to introduce irrational forces into the world, in the form of magic, astrology, and similar practices, was minimized in Judaism precisely because of its history of warfare against enemies with just such beliefs. Because Egypt had a death cult, Judaism reacted against worship of the dead (especially ancestor worship); because surrounding religions had fertility goddesses alongside their masculine deities, Judaism stressed the monotheistic power of its single, masculine deity.

There remained only one more step before Judaism could become a religion of world-transforming significance. It was narrowly focused upon the political aspirations of one particular ethnic group in the Middle East. To spread its influence, it had to become completely universal in its recruitment, bringing in everyone in the world as members. This is what Christianity did; Christianity has to be understood as a particular faction within this late period of ancient Judaism. After Babylon was overrun by the Persian empire (about 550 B. C.) the Jews were allowed to return home to Palestine, but they never regained full political independence. Their state was a client or puppet, first of the Persians, then of other large-scale empires, and eventually of the Romans. One faction in Jewish politics advocated guerilla warfare to make the prophecy come true and reestablish the state that Yahwe's prophets had predicted. Other factions, especially the Pharisees, held that the most important thing was religious behavior, and stressed that

Yahwe's support depended upon maintaining the old ritual purity. But the Pharisees stressed purity to the extreme that many of the Jews (especially those who lived far from Jerusalem, and could not participate in its temple rituals) were actually excluded. Christianity emerged as the opposite tendency within Judaism. It proposed, against the guerilla warriors, that the kingdom of Yahwe, the kingdom of God, was not to be merely the reestablishment of the little state of David and Solomon, but was to encompass the whole earth. It was still to be a worldly kingdom, but raised to a nearly transcendent level, given that it meant the end of the Roman empire and could happen only at the end of history, the end of the world. The early Christians did indeed think that the end of the world was near.

Against the Pharisees, the Christian Jews argued that the old ritual purity had to be relaxed, that the old covenant with Yahwe should be considered open so that everyone who truly believed should be allowed to join. At this point, it was still a movement within Judaism. The Christians believed that because there is only one God, all people should become His worshipers. Everyone should be invited to join the chosen people, to become Jews, but not in any restricted, ethnic sense. The Pharisees, on the other hand, held to the path of ritual purity developed in the time of the Babylonian exile. The two positions were still open at the time of Jesus. It is only in the next generation, when Christianity embarked on an energetic campaign to convert the gentiles, under the leadership of Paul, that a showdown occurred. The Pharisees called Paul to the temple in Jerusalem to account for his heresy; the outcome was that the Christians and the Pharisees mutually excommunicated each other, so to speak. From this time forward, there would be not two factions of Judaism, but Christians and Jews. A few years later, in 66 A. D., the guerilla warriors in Palestine made their last desperate effort at independence, and were crushed by the Roman army. The temple at Jerusalem was destroyed, and with it the aim of reestablishing the kingdom of Israel. Henceforth Jews were distributed abroad. Christianity was cut loose entirely from its Jewish political roots, to make its own way in transforming the Western world.

THE RELIGION OF INDIA

Weber frequently compared ancient Judaism, and indeed the entire ancient Near Eastern world, with India. Mystical religions had appeared in both places, and there were signs of something like a caste system developing in the Near East as well. The increasing social segregation of the Jews through their emphasis on ritual purity vis-à-vis outsiders, Weber felt, was a movement headed in the direction of a caste system. Nevertheless the Mediterranean went a different route, leading to Christianity and to activist, world-transforming capitalism, while India followed the path to ascetic withdrawal into mystical contemplation in the religious sphere and all that this implied regarding the lack of a religious transformation of the world.

India, then, is one of Weber's crucial comparisons. He began by pointing out that India had many social conditions favorable to capitalism. It was a land of trade, with a high development of handicrafts and occupational specialization. Merchants were not crushed by an overwhelming state nor heavily burdened by taxes, but constituted an autonomous stratum, with their own guilds corresponding to those of medieval Europe. Loans and other financial instruments for longdistance trade were available, and state credit, tax farming, and other government fiscal policies paralleled those in the West. India was the place where the basis of rational calculability, arithmetic based on the positional number system (including the use of zero), had been invented. (This is the number system we now use, though we incorrectly call it "Arabic numerals"; it supplanted the clumsy Roman numerals or the still clumsier Greek system of using letters of the alphabet as numbers). Especially in the classic age of medieval India (approximately 500 B. C. to 600 A. D.), India was a land of wealthy, mercantile cities, a booming economy, with a degree of rationalization that led the world. Why didn't capitalism achieve its breakthrough there?

Weber argues that because the economic conditions were generally favorable, the obstacle to capitalism is to be found elsewhere, especially in the realm of social ideals and of religion. He proposes a culprit: the caste system, and the religious values that supported it. But how did this system arise? The caste system did not simply come down from the ancient Vedic period (before 100 B.C.) when wandering Aryan tribes migrated to India from the northwest. The religious system at that time was organized around animal sacrifices and presided over by priests, the Brahmans. The rigidity of the caste system, with its elaborate belief that contact among different castes was defiling to the higher groups, developed only gradually, and reached its full bloom in precisely the medieval period when urban conditions for an economic takeoff were most ripe. This was a period of social change, when the old sacrificial religion of the Vedas (the ancient religious hymns) was changed into the mysticism of yoga, and later into the prayer-worship of savior-gods such as Krishna and Shiva. It was also a time of conflict, as Hinduism was challenged by new religions, Buddhism and Jainism, which denied the caste system and proposed a way to overcome its central problem of reincarnation through endless lives in the world. In the end, Jainism was reduced to a minor sect, and Buddhism was driven out of India almost entirely. The question for Weber was: Why did the caste system and orthodox Hinduism triumph, and thus turn aside the possibility of the transformation to capitalism?

There are four main castes mentioned in the medieval texts. The Brahmans were the priests; the Kshatriyas were the warriors and kings; the Vaishyas were merchants, farm-owners, and craftsmen; the Shudras were laborers, servants, and slaves. The important point about the caste system, however, was that it was capable of a certain dynamism. It could be extended to new social groups, and the four large castes could split into subcastes with their own rankings. Brahmans did not always remain priests; many of them became wealthy landowners, others became scribes, still others cooks (who alone could prepare ritually pure foods in the homes of wealthier Brahmans). Kshatriyas, too, spread into different occupations, including Buddhist or Jaina monks. The Vaishyas, or middle class, and the Shudras, or workers, split into an especially large number of subcastes, corresponding to many different occupations. This was so characteristic that Weber compared these subcastes to guilds or trade unions. Finally, there were also people from outside the caste system, such as pagan tribes from the jungles or hills on the fringe of Indian civilization. The caste system regarded these tribal peoples as especially impure, and kept them at a great distance. Hence they were "untouchables," and in effect made into castes anyway, even though they did not accept the Hindu religion that legitimated the system.

Weber compares castes to a number of other forms of social organization, in order to isolate the peculiarity of the caste system, as well as the causal conditions that underlie its origin and expansion. Castes might appear to be like tribes, and one hypothesis is that the Aryan invaders of India conquered dark-skinned natives, whom they eventually incorporated into their own society as the lower caste of Shudras. Weber admits that there is an element of this in the history of castes. But it cannot be the full explanation, because the three upper castes are all parts of the same Aryan tribes. Moreover, a tribe is a political association, with its own territory and its obligations of blood revenge for killing of its members by outsiders. Castes are not political units, nor are they confined to a particular territory, but crosscut these boundaries. The crucial social characteristics of a caste are endogamy, the rule of in-marriage (or at least marriage kept restricted with certain social groups); dietary rules requiring strict commensalism, so that members of a higher caste cannot eat with caste outsiders; and ritual standards that keep a caste pure only by keeping its distance from other castes. None of these hold for an entire tribe, although tribes that lose their territory, Weber says, are on their way to becoming castes if they also acquire these additional traits of ritual concern for group purity.

Castes (and especially subcastes) also tend to be occupational specialties or monopolies. This suggests that their basis is economic. But it is a peculiar way of dividing the occupational structure. Weber compares castes to the guilds that existed in medieval European cities. The main difference is that castes are hereditary, whereas guilds in the European sense are not. Furthermore, India also had guilds in its cities of the classic period, when it approached capitalism. In the rural villages, there were no guilds, but the different occupations were rigidly apportioned to various subcastes: one had a monopoly on carrying water, another on building brick walls, another on weaving, and so forth. This was a major reason, Weber proposed, why the caste system spread and established itself firmly in the period when the economy was growing. Why should members of the lower social ranks adopt the caste system? It put them in a position far below the Brahmans and Kshatriyas, and made them objects of social dishonor, to be shunned and kept at a distance. But the caste system also had something to offer (in addition to the promises of the reincarnation doctrine, which will be discussed below). It created the strongest possible trade unions. Each line of work was religiously legitimated and made inviolable to outsiders. This economic incentive in the form of caste monopolies was no doubt the major reason for the voluntary spread of the caste system.

In the cities of medieval India, the castes were less strong than in the villages, and instead the merchants and craftsmen there were organized into guilds more like the European pattern. These urban groups were much more favorable to Buddhism and Jainism, and hence had a tendency to reject the caste system anyway. Why then did they not go all the way in the European direction? Let us see just what this would have meant. Weber stressed that a crucial characteristic of the Western city was that it became an independent political unit, based on a coalition of its leading members. "Citizenship" is precisely this belonging to a little local republic, the members of the city banded together for their mutual aid and defense. Early instances of this were found in the city-states of ancient Greece, where members of the citizen army shared political rights. Again in the European Middle Ages, these self-armed and locally self-ruling cities sprang up in northern Italy, Germany, the Netherlands, and elsewhere. For Weber, they provided a major basis for the later development of capitalism, by helping establish a legal and political system favorable to bourgeois business interests. The modern Western state is a combination of the bureaucracy of the centralizing kings with the citizenship rights established in the self-governing cities.

But Indian cities never became independent, nor (after some very early beginnings) were they ever republics, coalitions of citizens who defended themselves militarily and made their own laws. Indian cities were merely administrative seats for the rulers, and places where markets existed. Weber put his finger on the crucial difference between Indian and Western cities. The medieval European cities were coalitions of guilds, because the guilds were not ritually exclusive to each other. They fraternized regularly, holding religious feasts in which representatives of all the guilds took part; and on the basis of this religious organization, they formed oath-bound political organizations for self-defense and self-rule. Christianity had this facilitating role for medieval European civic organization. Earlier, the Greek civic cults similarly brought about a coalition of the families that made up an ancient city.

But in India, the guilds that controlled the economic life of the cities never established any organization linking them together. Insofar as the Hindu religion and its caste system continued to be influential, it reinforced ritual barriers between the different subcastes. Therefore even the wealthy merchants could not turn their resources into political power, because their religiously legitimated subdivisions kept them from achieving a collective organization. There remains one more possibility. Why didn't the anti-Hindu religions, Buddhism and Jainism, do this for them? Both of these broke down caste barriers, taking their converts from all ranks of society. The trouble is, these religions went too far in denying the relevance of the ordinary activities of the world. Buddhism and Jainism were religions of monks, who gave up all property and retired to engage in meditation. Strictly speaking, there was no Buddhist or Jaina church; pious laypersons might gain some religious merit by giving alms to the begging monks, but they themselves could never achieve salvation in Nirvana unless they gave up their occupations and became monks themselves. By contrast, the social significance of Christianity was that it left its followers in the world, where the church and its rituals could be used to create secular forms of social organization (such as the religious fraternities of the European cities).

Buddhism and Jainism had another political liability as well. Both were extremely pacifist, with strong religious taboos against the taking of life. Jainism was so extreme in this regard that Jaina monks wore gauze masks over their mouths, lest they injure an insect by accidentally breathing it in, and carried a broom to sweep their path lest they step on a living creature. This pacifism, Weber pointed out, made the Jaina followers suited only for urban occupations because there was too much destruction of animals in farming; thus Jainas tended to live in urban areas, to engage in commerce, and even to become rich. But neither they nor the Buddhists were capable of organizing a self-armed coalition of urban burghers, such as that which provided the basis for the independent cities of Europe, or the city-states of ancient Greece. This comparison enables Weber to show exactly how important Christianity was for the distinctive development of the West. It "shattered the ritual barriers against commensalism" and thus opened the way for "the cultic community of the citizens" (Weber, 1916-1917/1958c: 37, 36). Indian religion made this impossible, and hence it "steered India's social structure—which for a time apparently stood close to the threshold of European urban development—into a course that led it far away from any possibility of such development" (Weber, 1916-1917/1958c: 39).

The caste system had an important reflection in the realm of religious ideas. The central belief of Hinduism, in Weber's view, was the doctrine of *karma,* the belief in reincarnation: Everyone lives numerous lives, both in the past and in the future. Where one is now, whether high caste or low, human or animal, depends on what one has done in past lives. Good behavior brings a better rebirth in the next life, bad behavior a demotion to a lower level. Weber regarded this as an almost perfect explanation for the sufferings of ordinary life, with an accompanying religious promise of how matters are recompensed in the future. Any social injustice is a just desert for one's past sins, and the privileges of the rich and powerful are rewards for their accumulation of good karma from their past. This not only justifies the social order, but also promises that one can work toward a better position in future lives. Further, the doctrine reinforces and perpetuates the caste system, because the most important duties that determine whether one accumulates good or bad karma, are one's caste duties. The member of a low caste who observes the proper taboos, who keeps the proper distance and respects the higher castes, is told he will be rewarded by a rebirth in a higher caste. Women, who are regarded as low ranking within their own castes, can hope to be reborn as men, if they properly accept their subordinate position in this lifetime. On the other hand, if members of the higher castes, the Brahmans and Kshatriyas, fail to maintain ritual purity and allow themselves to be defiled by the lower castes, they will fall from their high rank in future lifetimes. The doctrine of reincarnation thus serves to keep everyone maintaining all the caste taboos, and the rigid segregation and ceremonial deference that makes up the caste system.

Weber comes very close to saying that the reincarnation doctrine is an ideology, in the Marxian sense, covering up and justifying the raw stratification of power, prestige, and wealth that make up the social reality of caste in the real world. But as a comparative sociologist, he has an admiration for the sheer intellectual consistency of the system. Provided one does not question whether there is any future life at all, the reincarnation doctrine provides a perfect theodicy, explaining why there is evil in the world, as well as providing a way out of it. The doctrine is flexible, capable of extension to all situations, of adding new subcastes, and of justifying any change in social circumstances. If a high caste loses power (such as by political or even religious revolution), this can be explained as being the result of sins in past lives: And who can really disprove it? Buddhism can be regarded as punishment brought on the Hindus for having committed ritual sins; and Buddha came to be regarded as merely one of the lesser incarnations of the Hindu god Vishnu. It is a doctrine that legitimates everything, by including it somewhere in the endless wheels of reincarnation. The yoga doctrine could come into Hinduism, as well, even though it was a kind of "shortcut" technique for directly escaping all the reincarnations. Through yoga one could immediately reach the highest religious stage of Nirvana or, in the theistic versions, of union with the highest god. The practice of yoga, in the orthodox doctrine, was reserved for members of the highest caste; only after having carried out one's caste duties at lower levels for many lifetimes could one be reborn at the social position where one could actually become a holy yogin.

Weber argued that a doctrine that solved so many religious problems so neatly must be the product of intellectuals. He referred to it as a form of rationalization, because it provided a highly consistent way of viewing the world. (Recall that in Chapter 4 we found that this is the core meaning of "rationality" in Weber's usage.) The karma doctrine is not a product of economic conditions, in the Marxian sense that it merely springs directly from the economic interests of a particular class. Instead, it must have been produced by intellectual specialists, concerned with rational ethical thought, in this case, the Brahmans (Weber, 1916-1917/1958c: 121, 11). With this reservation, however, Weber goes on to portray Indian religion in general as highly congruent with the interests of the secular society. The Brahmans were the carriers of this religious ethic, and it fitted in well with their own social situation. It exalted their status honor to the highest position and protected it against attack. The rulers, too, accepted the Hindu religious structure insofar as it legitimated their own political position. This was not without some variation; Weber points out that when the rulers were most powerful and could build centralized bureaucratic states, they tended to repudiate Hinduism and support the Buddhists or Jainas. This was because Brahmans were tied to the existing upper classes, always the main threat to an absolutist ruler. Hence it was useful to acquire an alternative form of legitimation. Buddhism filled this role (ironically, in view of its avowed pacifism) both in the large conquest states that occasionally developed in India itself, and especially by spreading to the kingdoms emerging in Ceylon, Tibet, Central and Southeast Asia, and Japan. But the political history of India was mostly rather decentralized, and power was fragmented among numerous smaller states. A decentralized aristocracy dominated most of the time, which favored the more traditional religious legitimation of the Brahmans.

The caste system, the religious doctrines of Brahman Hinduism, and the political structure of India thus meshed into a mutually reinforcing pattern. The economic developments of the cities of medieval India, which Weber felt had so much potential for producing modern capitalism, were turned aside. Instead, India became the land of tradition, a social order that was fundamentally unshakable. Political upheavals and the encounter with new societies from outside could do no more than add new refinements to the caste system.

THE RELIGION OF CHINA

Historically, China had numerous social conditions that were similar to those of Europe. Some of these were favorable to the development of modern capitalism, others were obstacles. From as early as the Han dynasty (ca. 200 B.C.-200 A.D.), China was a land of cities. There was a flourishing long-distance trade. Cities had autonomous, self-regulating guilds of merchants and handicrafts. These conditions generally suggested a favorable outlook for capitalism. At the same time, the monetary system was chaotic, consisting of many different currencies (and long periods when no coined or paper money was used at all, but instead bolts of silk were used as a standard of exchange). China had a bureaucratic government structure in the strong dynasties, but it did not provide the necessary regularity for capitalist markets because it was only partially bureaucratized. Weber referred to it as an instance of patrimonial bureaucracy, a combination of impersonal bureaucratic offices with personal and familistic politics. From this combination came the tendency to "corrupt" officials, the bribes, self-enrichment, and behind-the-scenes dealings that seemed so characteristic to Westerners of Oriental governments. In these circumstances, there could be no rational economic policy of the state.

Nevertheless, Weber pointed out that many of these negative features also existed in medieval and early modern Europe. Given that they were overcome in the West, they did not necessarily constitute an insuperable obstacle to the rise of rational capitalism. At least, he comments, China had the advantage of a strong state, over long periods of time, which pacified the entire area and avoided the predatory relations and destructiveness of feudal warfare that prevailed in Europe.

The major structural obstacles to capitalism, in Weber's view, were three: (1) The Chinese city was an administrative center of government, and a place for markets. But it was not a city in the Western sense, ruled by a body of citizens. Self-governing and rule-making assemblies did not exist in China. Like the Indian city, the Chinese city was divided into smaller groups (in this case among family clans rather than castes) who could not overcome the barriers among themselves to establish a civic coalition; hence the lack of independent power for bourgeois interests and their representation in the law.

(2) The Chinese kinship system never got beyond the point of sharp separation between internal and external group ethics. Chinese villages were typically organized around a single clan (which Weber referred to by the term "sib") held together by ancestor worship. The same clan

structure prevailed in the cities too, with different clans living in different districts, sometimes separated by walls; thus making Chinese cities like a collection of villages right next to each other. These clans had strong internal ties. The family temple also served as a school, a bank, a pawnshop, even a storehouse. The clan's elders were responsible for taxes, and for care of local roads and other public works. The clan assembled capital and would loan funds to its own members. But its economic functions were sharply limited by the division between insiders and outsiders. Clan members were supposed to take care of each other because of family solidarity, not out of concern for profit; hence loans and other economic investments were made without interest, in order to maintain the group. On the other hand, economic dealings with outsiders were covered by no ethical obligations at all. One could maximize profits, cheat, and engage in sharp dealings with a good conscience, given that the ethical rules only decreed obligations of good behavior among family members.

This was the opposite of the situation in Christian Europe, which Weber believed was most sharply represented by the Puritans. The crucial message of Christianity was to reduce the place of family, to make family members no more important in terms of ethical obligations than any other human beings. The Christian doctrine of the universal brotherhood of mankind thus allowed the extension of ethics to business dealings with the outsiders, while eliminating the privileged position of relatives from business profit seeking. The prevailing Chinese religion did the opposite. Confucianism summed up ethical obligations in four relationships: between father and son, older brother and younger brother, husband and wife, ruler and subordinate. All these relationships were hierarchic. The lower-ranking person owed reverence and obedience to the higher ranking; at the same time, the higher-ranking person had the obligation to reciprocate for this loyalty by taking care of his subordinates. (The masculine pronoun is deliberate; Confucianism is explicitly sexist, and does not envision women as ever being formally superior or even equal to men.)

Notice that all of these relationships are in the family, except for one: that between ruler and ruled. This epitomized the structure of Chinese society. The family, in the form of the large clan, was its basis. Above these clans was a thin layer of bureaucratic officials forming the state. Hierarchic relationships (at least in theory) predominated everywhere. There was no room for horizontal relationships, such as professions, self-governing assemblies, or the laws of the market.

(3) The third obstacle was the lack of an independent, rational legal system. By this Weber meant a codified law administered on a regular basis by a professional stratum of jurists. The Chinese dynasties had their laws, of course. But they were not codified and worked out in an intellectually consistent fashion. Especially lacking were the rules and regulations concerning property and economic transactions that would have been necessary for the development of modern capitalism. What laws did exist were the administrative pronouncements of the government, reflecting whatever policy happened to be in effect at the time. On a more long-run philosophical basis, there was Confucianism. But this stressed that good order was maintained by upholding the basic family relationships and by correct ritual behavior. It put what it considered to be the correct ethical policies ahead of the rational analysis of particular economic and legal issues in their own terms.

The main purpose of Weber's *Religion of China* was to show how its distinctive religious outlook helped to keep it from developing capitalism. Religion is implicated in all three of the obstacles enumerated above, because all three of them are tied directly or indirectly to Confucianism and the family cults. Interestingly enough, though Weber from time to time stressed the independent effect of religious ideas upon economic development, he also provided an extensive sociological analysis of the conditions under which religious ideas are themselves produced.

For example, the basic structure of Chinese society was heavily influenced by geographical conditions. China is a river-valley civilization. From very early in its history, its social organization was formed around irrigation, canals, flood-control, and other water-works. This gave impetus to forming a centralized bureaucratic state. In this respect China resembled the social structure of Egypt. Weber draws an interesting religious consequence from this. Not only is the state centralized quite early, before traditions of independent powers arise in either the political or economic spheres, the Emperor himself rules with a religious charisma, which Weber argues derives from the nature-magic of primitive societies. Just as primitive magicians were believed to be able to read omens, to carry out rituals ensuring fertility, and to fend off natural disasters, the Emperor of the early river-valley kingdom carried out rituals that ensured good harvests, guarded against floods, and kept nature as well as society in order.

This routinization of the magical charisma of nature-controlling rituals was the foundation of the Chinese religious tradition. The

Emperor was worshiped, not as a god, but as a human link with the powers of heaven. As long as the Emperor carried out the proper rituals and observed the correct behavior, the land would be prosperous. Lower ranking officials acquired their legitimacy because some portion of this nature-magic of the Emperor was passed down to them. They too were supposed to be exemplars of correct behavior, rather than mere secular administrators. From this came the Chinese tradition of propriety in manners, which was taken as the central duty of the ruling classes.

Confucianism rationalized this system of government by nature-magic within a centralized bureaucratic state. By the time of the Han dynasty (and following conflicts with rival philosophical factions), the Confucians got themselves established as the main administrators of the state bureaucracy. Confucianism became the official religion, or ideology, of the government. It added an ethical component to the original nature-magic; it was maintaining correct social relationships, as well as carrying out the proper ceremonies, that upheld the world order. There even developed a radical side of Confucianism, which said that the Emperor had the mandate of heaven, but only as long as he maintained correct behavior and looked after the prosperity of the people. If the Emperor failed to do this, then he had lost the mandate of heaven, and it was proper to rebel and establish a new emperor.

Weber compared the Confucians to the Puritans of Christianity. Both, he pointed out, are oriented toward the world, rather than toward a mystical withdrawal into the transcendental realm. The individual works out his or her salvation here below, by maintaining strict self-control and performing the right behaviors. Both religions were ascetic, opposing drunkenness, indulgence in orgiastic sex, and other "irrational" pleasure seeking. But the direction of this worldly task was radically different in the two cases. The Puritans subdued themselves in order to bring the world into harmony with God's will; theirs was an activist asceticism, which harnessed religious energies into a force that created modern capitalism. Confucianism provided no such leverage point to change the world. Its aim was not change at all, but to maintain a traditional order. Whereas Puritanism always had a radical and utopian component, Confucianism was conservative, looking backward to an ideal society of the past. Its highest aim was to uphold the familistic structure of society, Puritanism's to remake the whole world into a religious brotherhood.

Confucianism was also structurally responsible for the failure of China to develop a rationalized legal system. The Confucians were a class of government officials, not priests. There was no independent church of Confucianism (though temples to Confucius were eventually established). This was important, Weber believed, because in the West it was out of the conflict between church and state that an independent profession of lawyers emerged. In medieval Europe, the universities developed as part of the struggle for power between the papacy and the secular rulers; and it was there that traditions of legal scholarship developed. At the same time, the other "classical" professions emerged: medicine, theology, teaching, each with its own codified intellectual system, and its corporate organization and distinctive status. Nothing like this happened in China, because the intellectual stratum was simply absorbed into the state. Laws remained an arm of the government. For this reason, Weber believed, China did not develop an intellectual tradition of natural science either. Neither a conception of independent laws governing human affairs, nor the idea of scientific laws governing the cosmos, could get free of the Confucian worldview. Its basic conception always reduced intellectual questions to matters of correct ritual harmony, an offshoot of the original nature-magic at the basis of the legitimacy of the Chinese state.

To be sure, Confucianism was not the only religion in the history of China. Ignoring most of the early rival sects (before the time of the Han dynasty), Weber examined Taoism and Buddhism. Taoism was no challenge to the basic Confucian worldview. It too was a kind of nature-magic, but in this case rationalized by intellectuals into mysticism and aestheticism. In this form, it was easy enough for Confucian officials to harmonize Taoism with their official beliefs. When an official was in service to the government, he acted as a proper Confucian, maintaining the proper rituals and upholding social order. In private life, upon retirement or failure to achieve a position (or possibly political disgrace in the factional changes of politics), he could retire to his country estate and practice Taoism, by mystical contemplation, writing poems, and aesthetically contemplating nature. There was also a popular Taoism, which had priests and temples patronized by the lower classes. But this form of religion, Weber argued, provided no religious leverage at all for changing the world, after the fashion of Christianity. Popular Taoism was not an ethical religion at all, but a form of magic, selling omens and good-luck charms, magically curing illnesses, and promising long life or even physical immortality from fantastic pills and potions. In Weber's view, Buddhism played a similar role in Chinese life. (It is true that Weber devoted relatively little attention to Buddhism and did not seem to be very well informed on the role that it played, especially in medieval China, when it was a more powerful force for economic growth. This is one of the weaknesses of Weber's analysis; see Collins, 1986: chap. 3.)

On the whole, Weber depicts Chinese society as semirationalized. It achieved some important elements of rationalization fairly early in its history. It achieved the most thorough breakthrough to the bureaucratic state, pacified large territories, and promoted urban development and large-scale trade. Its dominant religion, too, gave a rather rationalized view of the world, in the sense that it was consistently worked out by religious intellectuals, the Confucians, and it made worldly activity rather than mystical escape its predominant focus. But this same structure compromised with the old family system and with nature-magic. Chinese bureaucracy and Confucianism incorporated these older forms, and made them the fundamental building blocks for the unchanging order it was trying to uphold. The paradoxical effect of the "modern" elements in Chinese society, Weber seems to be saying, was that they made the "premodern" forms permanent, and thus reinforced them as obstacles to the full development of modern capitalism.

7

Weber's Sociological Encyclopedia

ECONOMY AND SOCIETY

Weber's *Economy and Society* (1922/1968) is an enormous work of almost 1500 pages. For a long time it was known in the English-speaking world only in bits and pieces. Five different books have come out of it, each giving a somewhat different emphasis. These translations were part of the struggle over which interpretation of Weber would prevail: as either the neo-idealist sociologist of rationalization or as the materialist conflict theorist. Talcott Parsons (who had set off the battle by translating *The Protestant Ethic* in 1930), with his collaborators, translated Weber's introductory definitions as *The Theory of Social and Economic Organization* (1947); Edward Shils and Max Rheinstein produced a volume entitled *Max Weber on Law in Economy and Society* (1954), and Ephraim Fischoff produced *The Sociology of Religion* (1963). The other camp was led by Hans Gerth, who was also responsible for translating the volumes on China, India, and ancient Judaism in Weber's sociology of religion. Where Parsons et al. had concentrated on the most abstract definitions and on the more ideal institutions of religion and law, Gerth and C. Wright Mills, in a famous volume called *From Max Weber: Essays in Sociology* (1946), excerpted heavily from Weber's sociology of stratification and politics. This book contained Weber's famous pieces on bureaucracy and on class-status-

and-party, foundations of virtually all sociology courses on organizations and on stratification, respectively. Gerth's collaborator Don Martindale also translated *The City* (1958), from the latter part of *Economy and Society*, which deals with politics.

The "translation wars" came to an end in 1968, when the entire text of *Economy and Society* was finally brought out in English by Guenther Roth and Claus Wittich. Since that time, we have made some progress in putting together the pieces of Weber's work as a whole. But that cannot be all there is to it. The Germans of course had Weber's works available to them without the medium of translators all along; but for a long time Weber was ignored in Germany, or taken primarily as an idealist/ rationalist (which is the interpretation that still prevails there). And many American scholars have always been able to read Weber in the German original. The problem is more one of selection. Weber wrote prolifically, and even a single work such as *Economy and Society* calls for some principle of selection, some choice of a guiding theme by which to make sense of it. The translators who picked different aspects of Weber's work were making such a choice. It is only recently that we have begun to see that there are two sides to Weber, that they do not necessarily fit together well, but that both must be given their due.

In previous chapters of this book (Chapters 2, 3, and 4) I have already examined the idealist/rationalist side of Weber. What remains here is to look over *Economy and Society* from the point of view of what it contributes to a materialist conflict theory. In fact, it contributes a great deal. It is likely to have contributed even more had it been completed. Weber started writing the work in 1910 and then was interrupted by the war in 1914, after he had finished a draft of what is now Part II (the substantive part) of *Economy and Society*. In 1919-1920 he wrote the long set of definitions of the categories of sociological analysis, which make up the published Part I. But both parts were unfinished at the time of Weber's death.

Even as it stands, *Economy and Society* looks like an encyclopedia. As a matter of fact, it was designed to be part of a larger series that really *was* an encyclopedia. In 1909 Weber agreed to edit a new edition of the *Handbook of Political Economy*, an academic compilation that covered every area of economics. Recall that this was Weber's professional field; recall too that German economics was much broader than its modern American counterpart, and included not just the technical analysis of supply, demand, prices, production, employment, and so forth, but the entire historical and institutional structure associated with the economy, as well as the political and legislative questions that follow from this. In addition to lining up the other contributors (who included such luminaries as Joseph Schumpeter, Werner Sombart, and Emil Lederer), Weber took it upon himself to contribute part of a volume on the relationship between economy and society.

This work, which he never finished, became the opportunity for Weber to work out a comprehensive sociology. Because everything can be related to the economy, every topic in sociology would have to be treated. By the sheer amount of attention Weber gave to particular topics, one can gauge how important he thought it was in the overall scheme of things. We actually have his planned table of contents, which shows us what he would have done had he been able to finish the work. It is roughly like the *Economy and Society* that we have, but with certain notable differences in emphasis. For one thing, the work would not have been called *Economy and Society*, but *The Economy and the Social Orders and Powers (Die Wirtschaft und die gesellschaftlichen Ordnungen und Mächte)*. No doubt this is a clumsier title, and the first German editors of the manuscript were probably justified in picking a shorter and snappier one. But notice what Weber's own title stresses: Society is to be treated as two larger spheres, the "social orders" and "powers." The American translators, Roth and Wittich, left this title as the heading for Part II of *Economy and Society*, and rendered it in English as "The Economy and the Arena of Normative and De Facto Powers." This captures part of what Weber was talking about: "De facto powers" are precisely powers that are not legitimate, but are purely "the way it is," in American slang, what those with the ability to do so can get away with. That Weber would put this in his overall title indicates the extent to which he was willing to play up a realistic, even cynical, conflict theory in sociology. Thus a good bit of Weber's emphasis was censored by changing his main title to the blander *Economy and Society*. To be sure, Weber also referred to a second arena, social order. Nevertheless, to translate the other part of Weber's title as "the arena of normative ... powers," as Roth and Wittich did, is to place an emphasis on the normative side that is not actually there in Weber's own term. "*Ordnung*" means "order," and it has a very expressive, and also ambiguous, meaning in German. "*Alles in Ordnung!*" means "Everything is in order!" the kind of remark a drill sergeant might make when presenting his troops for inspection. It has a connotation of imposed order; although it also means order in the more abstract sense, and could simply refer to the way society is organized.

If we look at the table of contents as Weber actually published it in the prospectus for the whole economic encyclopedia, we can see that it corresponds roughly to the two parts of his title. Literally, what he writes is the following (Weber 1922/ 1968: lxvi; note that the headings in capitals are my own, to indicate how I think this falls into sections):

DEFINITIONS AND OVERVIEW
(1) Categories of the Various Forms of Social Order (*gesellschaftlicher Ordnung*).
    The Most General Relationships Between Economy and Society
    The Economic Relationships of Organized Groups

SOCIAL GROUPS
(2) Household, Oikos, and Enterprise
(3) Neighborhood, Kin Group, and Local Community
(4) Ethnic Group Relationships
(5) Religious Groups
    The Class Basis of the Religions; Complex Religions and Economic Orientation

THE ECONOMY
(6) The Market

POLITICS
(7) The Political Association
    The Social Determinants of Legal Development
    Status Groups, Classes, Parties
    The Nation
(8) Domination
    (a) The Three Types of Legitimate Domination
    (b) Political and Hierocratic Domination
    (c) Nonlegitimate Domination; the Typology of Cities
    (d) The Development of the Modern State
    (e) The Modern Political Parties

We can see that the outline has two big sections—social groups and politics—plus an introduction, and a discussion of the market in between them. This fits the two realms mentioned in Weber's title, the "social orders" and the "powers." The whole thing is to be started off by a treatment of categories; this is the chapter on definitions that burgeoned to over 300 pages and was published separately by Talcott Parsons. Then we have a series of different social groups: the household, the neighborhood, kinship, ethnic groups, and religious groups. Then comes a brief intermezzo on the market—that is, the economic realm to which all the rest is to be connected. (This remained only a tiny fragment, so we have to reconstruct from elsewhere what Weber really thought the economic market was like.) And finally, a set of very long chapters on politics.

The emphasis of the outline, and the amount of attention that Weber actually gave to each part, points to where he apparently thought "the action is" in sociology. Clearly enough, it is in politics. Chapters 2-5, on social groups (which are actually published as Chapters 2-6 of Part II of *Economy and Society*), are relatively modest, and make up a mere 60 pages, except for the book-length treatment of religious groups (235 pages). But the chapters on politics swell to over 735 pages in the American edition. It is here that Weber includes his sociology of law, the state, bureaucracy, and other forms of organization, as well as social groups (class, status group, party) that are the actors struggling for political power. Furthermore, this part of the work is far from finished. Weber was also going to write on the development of the modern state and modern political parties, and he was going to give a treatment of revolutions, with an analysis of the Russian Revolution and the revolutionary overthrow of the Kaiser in Germany, which happened just before Weber died.

It is really unfortunate that we don't have this part of Weber's work. Not only would it surely have been extremely illuminating as a sociological analysis of modern times, but it would have definitely shown Weber as a sociologist of politics and conflict. In my view, it would have given the preponderance, at least as far as Weber's actual contributions (and despite his methodological pronouncements), to the actual structure and struggles of groups in society, rather than to the effect of disembodied ideas on the world. His table of contents takes the hard-headed stance fairly explicitly. In referring to religions he makes his subheading *the class basis* of religions; his section on law is called *"the social determinants* of legal development." Notice too that he refers extensively to "nonlegitimate domination." In fact, that is his treatment of the city: self-rule by social groups. It is like saying that democracy is a struggle, and that as such it is not determined by the usual principles of legitimating ideals that prevail in authoritarian states. What he might have said about political parties and about revolution, I think, would have borne this out.

WEBER'S COMPARATIVE SOCIOLOGY
AS A SYSTEMATIC THEORY

Economy and Society explores one sociological topic after another in a kind of systematic tour of the field. Furthermore, because Weber was familiar with the broad range of world history, he treats each issue in terms of the generalizations that can be made on the basis of all the societies he knew about. Is it, let us say, a question of political organization? Weber then proceeds to show what the Chinese and the Egyptians had in common, how they resembled the bureaucratic states of modern Europe, how they differed from ancient Rome and from the Middle Ages of India, and so on. This is one reason reading *Economy and Society* is a mind-boggling experience for most people. The sheer knowledge of history that is summed up in sentences (or even parts of sentences) is usually intellectually overwhelming. Even professional historians tend to recoil; because their professional training has made them concentrate on a fairly narrow slice of space and time, they often report that the sensation of dealing with the Weberian style of comparison is dizzying.

Nevertheless, we ought to recognize that this is Weber's strength and our weakness, not vice versa. For comparisons are the basis of any science, and sociology can establish its most powerful generalizations only by seeing the conditions under which events occur. What sociology usually deals with are large-scale entities and processes: the forms of the state, democracy, revolution, religion, stratification, and so forth; we cannot see the major variations among them—and hence their causes— unless we can compare them as a whole, and that means comparing whole societies. Even the family, which we take for granted as a small-scale institution in our own society, cannot be understood in terms of why this particular family form exists today instead of something else, unless we make wide-ranging historical comparisons. That is the reason Weber is our major sociological theorist. It is not because he merely cogitated about categories and methodologies. He was basically an empiricist of a comparative sort. All his statements, including the methodological pronouncements that have been picked up by the anticomparativists (and antipositivists) of the discipline, are nevertheless grounded in his basic enterprise of comparing across the known range of human societies.

As the result of his comparison, Weber established some of the major dimensions of social organization. That is, he told us what are the most fruitful structures to look at. We will shortly examine some of these in a little more detail: the models of organization, the three-dimensional approach to stratification, the view of politics as a struggle that undergirds the rest of the social order. Why is it "fruitful" to focus on these? Because they are complexes that hang together in historical reality. They are, so to speak, "natural dividing lines" in the social landscape. But to recognize this is to at least implicitly admit there are certain causal complexes, certain major factors that cause other things to take a certain pattern around them. Weber tended to refer to his analysis of such basic factors and related complexes of social order as "ideal types." As we have seen, he created this terminology, fairly early in his career, in order to establish a middle ground between sheer historical narration as an endless set of particulars, and the sorts of causal models that disregarded empirical variations. In his methodological pronouncements, Weber was always a historicist, someone who proclaimed that history as it unfolds is always unique, and that one cannot generalize about it, but only interpret it. Nevertheless, Weber's major comparative works, and above all *Economy and Society*, do much more than that. They actually provide a set of theories, causal models of organization, stratification, politics, and so on. The ideal types themselves, established as they are by a comparison of patterns common to many historical societies, contain these theories. The comparative method on which they are based provides the science, even though it is not what Weber himself consciously intended.

It is for this reason that Weber is our greatest sociologist, and *Economy and Society* is his greatest book. For if he were nothing more than what he declared he was, an interpreter of the myriad particular paths of history, he would hardly have been an inspiration and a guide for the discipline of sociology. It is true that historical sociology has enjoyed a certain popularity in the past few decades, but the bulk of sociologists deal with the institutions of modern society, and relatively few of them (especially before about 1965) have dealt much with history. Weber would be a rather esoteric specialist if his work did not have a generalizing appeal. And indeed, why should we plow through his complicated references to Islamic society, China, Persia, medieval Europe and all the rest if there were no other payoff than understanding what is unique about each of these? In fact, there is a payoff of a very important sort. Weber established the basis of the sociology of organizations, stratification, and politics. Because all other social institutions can be analyzed in terms of these, most of the rest of sociology takes a certain amount of guidance from the theoretical perspective that emerges from Weber's work. Empirical studies of modern American (or British, French, or any other) society have thus built a body of knowledge the outlines of which are essentially Weberian.

WEBER'S THEORY OF STRATIFICATION

Weber presents his main discussion of the theory of stratification in the midst of his political sociology. This has caused certain problems with understanding it. The model is famous under the title "Class, Status Group, and Party": the three-dimensional view of stratification. Classes are economic groupings—roughly what Marx and Engels had in mind, although Weber adds some refinements. They are groups of people who have a similar position on an economic market. As such, classes are merely statistical categories. They are not real groups, in the sense of people who feel they belong together, who actually associate together, and who have a name—a social identity—for themselves collectively. This latter type of group is what Weber calls a "status group."

Finally, there are political parties. This part of the model muddies the picture a bit, given that we are strictly concerned with stratification, for parties are added because Weber here was discussing politics. To be exact, he was discussing who the actors are in politics, the groups that struggle for power. His answer was three kinds of groups: economic classes and their economic interests, status groups (for instance, ethnic groups), and, finally, parties. Parties, Weber says, live "in the house of power," by which he means that they are groups actually organized for political action. The distinction among class, status group, and party is analytical rather than concrete. They are not mutually exclusive; the same individual—or for that matter the same group—could belong to all three at the same time. Let us put it this way: a class could get itself formed into a status group, and both a class and a status group could then become organized as a political party. Then again, each of these could occur separately. There are classes that are not status groups, status groups (for example, ethnic groups) that do not coincide with classes and have not formed parties, and parties that are autonomous. For instance, within the structure of a government, there may be many different organizational factions, which act as "parties" in the struggle for power.

Weber's approach is particularly useful for understanding pluralistic situations in which stratification is complicated by overlapping groups, and the struggle for political power is also factionalized. For instance, Catholics versus Protestants versus Jews as status groups may crosscut social classes; so may blacks versus white Euro-Americans versus Chicanos versus Orientals. And political parties may have an organization of their own, so that they pursue their own interests (keeping their politicians in power), which are not reducible to those of any particular group in the society around it, neither class nor status. Accordingly there has been a tendency to treat Weber's theory as being mainly designed for situations with this kind of pluralism, and even to see it as an attempt to reduce the Marxian insight about class conflict into a morass of pluralistic superficialities. But this is a misreading of Weber. A pluralistic situation is only one of the ways in which his model is applicable. Remember, it is an analytical model: Weber presents three types of groups, but does not say what the relationship among class, status group, and party must necessarily be. We must add a theory to it to predict when they will be maximally crosscutting in the pluralistic fashion, and when they will be arranged otherwise.

For one thing, they might all be organized around social classes. Weber's classes are only statistical categories: people who have the same relationship to the economic situation because they have the same position on the market. People who sell their labor (the working class) versus those who buy their labor (the employing or capitalist class) is one such major division. Weber also has two other class divisions, which are less familiar to the Marxists: the division between those who lend money and those who are their debtors, and the division between sellers and consumers. Weber points out that class conflict on these dimensions, too, has been important in world history, not merely the employer/ worker conflict that Marx focused upon. For simplicity's sake, I will leave out these other types here and concentrate on capitalists versus workers.

Economic classes consist of people who may all act in a similar way—for example, vote for the same economic interests in politics, have certain attitudes, and so forth. But they do not necessarily constitute a

real group, a community. Here Weber parallels a problem that greatly
concerned Marx and Engels: the creation of class consciousness. Weber
provides the solution: a class becomes class conscious when it turns into
a status group. Above, I used the example of ethnic and religious groups
(Catholics, Protestants, Jews, Chicanos) to represent status groups. But
an even more common form of status group is actually based on social
class. What, for instance, do we mean by "high society" (sometimes just
called "Society," in the sense of the "Society pages" in the newspaper)?
These social gatherings of rich people represent the process by which
they turn their wealth into a group culture, a sense of their collective
identity. Status groups (at least in the upper ranks) typically idealize
economic classes; they build a lifestyle and a community organization
out of their wealth. They also use it as their claim to social eminence, as if
to say, "We are distinguished people, not because we are rich—what a
vulgar thing to say!—but because we attend charity banquets and art
museum openings, hold very polite dinner parties, and present our
daughters at debutante balls where they will meet only the nicest young
men, and not end up marrying some 'nobody' who lacks our distinguished lifestyle."

Weber would call this the process of legitimation, this cloaking of
oneself in claims based on the honorableness of one style of life. Here we
see one difference between Weber's view of social classes turning into
status groups, and Marx and Engels's theory of the rise of class
consciousness. For Marx and Engels, the main concern was how the
subordinate class, especially the working class in the capitalist era, could
get itself together to achieve consciousness of itself as a revolutionary
force. Weber, on the other hand, stresses that it is the upper classes who
are most likely to form tightly organized status groups. That is one of
their main advantages in the class struggle for social domination. The
upper classes are better organized and they put more into legitimating
themselves. What the Marxians would refer to as "false consciousness"
on the part of the workers is mainly the way they are bedazzled by the
trappings of the upper class, and take them as some kind of superior
beings to be at least grudgingly admired, rather than as enemies to be
overthrown. This is not to say that only the higher classes become
organized as status groups. It is possible for all classes to do so, though
the upper class is most likely to achieve a status group structure that
coincides with their entire class, that mobilizes more or less all of them
into one structure. The middle class, too, tends to form its own
community, and so does the working class and the outcasts at the

bottom who form the lower class. But the lower groups in this ranking tend to form localistic communities, small groups of neighbors and relatives who have only a local consciousness, and whose boundaries are closed to the world around them, even to members of their own economic class who live at a distance.

In this respect, Weber leads into modern theory and research on social class. For further information, the reader is referred to my book *Conflict Sociology* (Collins, 1975: chap. 2). Here, I have space only to describe one more of Weber's contributions to the analysis of stratification. In the section of *Economy and Society* devoted to religious groups, he compresses a massive comparison of religions in the different societies of world history, and comes up with a picture of the basic religious tendencies of the various social classes. Weber's generalizations about religion and social class, I would suggest, give us a key to understanding the differences in the cultures of class stratification. And in fact, religions are extremely well suited to do so. For religions are organizations that encompass communities; they bring together congregations, groups of worshipers or meditators or ritualists. Religions provide these groups with a common outlook, and implicitly or explicitly with a set of moral principles or attitudes on how to live their lives. Hence religions make both social communities and their cultural outlooks. In Weber's terms, they create legitimation for the group and for the lifestyle that it pursues; thus they are a crucial basis for status groups, as well as for maintaining the status ranking by which some such groups dominate others.

From this point of view, what Weber says about the religious propensities of different social classes is extremely revealing. The upper classes will be discussed first. Weber (1922/1968: 472-477) points out that the military nobility throughout history has always had some kind of code of honor, which they usually couched in religious terms. They believed they were ordained by God to be knights, to fight crusades for the Christian God or for Islam's Allah, or simply because (in the Hindu religion) their caste duty was to fight and to rule. Religion for such classes is basically a means of justifying their domination. Not all ruling classes have been military; some of them have been bureaucratic elites, such as the mandarins of the Chinese dynasties, the officials of the late Roman empire, the office-aristocracy of Europe in the late Middle Ages. For them too, Weber points out, religion was treated as a matter of public policy. It was good for the state to promote religion, because religion represented good social order. The attitude of the Confucians was typical in this regard: They believed that carrying out the proper rituals was essential for maintaining society, but they themselves did not believe in any transcendental reality. This is a very "Establishment" attitude about religion, that it is a matter of good form and a useful thing for society, but not something to throw oneself into subjectively and with too much personal enthusiasm—that would be in bad taste, and rather too much like the lower classes (see below)! Now if we broaden the discussion beyond what Weber specifically says about religion, we can see that his model gives us the broad outlines of upper class culture generally. It is concerned with rituals and proper formalities, even if these may no longer be religious in a secular society like our own—but instead charity banquets, balls, and formal parties. It uses these things to legitimate themselves, to bring together their own community, and to indicate their superiority to others. But notice: they are not taken in by the rituals; for them, too much religious enthusiasm (or any other kind of enthusiasm) would be losing one's control, something that other social classes can give in to, but not the class in command.

The analysis now turns to the middle class. Weber (1922/1968: 481-484) is mostly summarizing evidence from premodern societies, so he finds this outlook among the small shopkeepers and craftsmen of the cities of the agrarian empires. It was in just this group within the Roman empire that Christianity developed. And, in fact, this epitomizes the religious outlook of the middle class, the "petite bourgeoisie": It is ascetic, moralistic, community oriented, respectable, and hardworking. It is suspicious of pleasures, especially of those in which one loses control of oneself (sex, gambling, intoxication). It maintains a rigid control over the individual, but tries to do so in an internalized, psychological way. Here religion plays an important part, by moralizing these injunctions of lower-middle class lifestyle, and making them into the path to salvation. On the secular level, the salvation is really from the hard economic realities of this class position. Small business people maintain a precarious respectability, subject to market forces that at any time can wipe out their capital and plunge them into the depths of the working class (from which many of them may in fact have just risen). Hence moralistic religion is often adopted anticipatorily by working-class people who are striving by their own efforts to pull themselves up across the class line. In the modern world, the size of this lower-middle-class group has grown to include lower clerical employees, skilled workers (plumbers, electricians, and so forth) who own their own businesses and similar positions. The relevance of Weber is not only that the same tendency toward a puritanical, moralistic religion is still found in this group; but that even when these groups are not religious, they still have the same kinds of attitudes in secular form. They believe in the "gospel of hard work," they complain about the immorality and dissoluteness of the society around them, both of the idlers of the higher classes (especially the hedonism of wealthier youth) and of the diabolical evils of the lower classes (in modern form, usually perceived as chiseling welfare recipients and racial minority street gangs). Like the early Christians, or similar groups also found in urban Islam, parts of India, and elsewhere, members of today's lower-middle class regard themselves as islands of righteousness in a world where everyone else has gone to the devil.

Working-class culture, for Weber (1922/1968: 468-472, 484-486), is found in the religious propensities of both modern manual laborers and factory workers, as well as in the historically earlier culture of peasants and farm laborers. All of these are near the bottom of the social structure, but not at the very bottom. (That is the lower class, which will be discussed next.) They usually constitute the majority of their society, and they do the work that provides the material conditions for everyone else. Weber points out that these classes have been essentially worldly in their religious attitudes. Moralistic and ascetic religions have never been strong in these groups. Their religions are episodic rather than continuous; instead of the steady psychological pressures characteristic of the lower-middle class, with its incessant search to hold onto respectability, religion for the working class is more intermittent. It consists of periodic festive occasions in which the local group is brought together to celebrate a wedding or a funeral (which despite its initial mournfulness, can often turn into a drinking bout). Religion itself is used for emotional release and worldly ends, such as bringing good luck, good health, curing sickness, or predicting the future. Working-class religion is often connected with magic, with "miracles" of the sort featured today in the tabloid press. All this has its historical counterpart, Weber shows, in the rural pagan religions, with their seasonal festivals and fertility rites. One could add that in our secular modern society, we have elaborated a set of rituals that take up so much attention, especially of working-class people, in the collective identities connected with spectator sports.

Finally, there is the group at the very bottom, the outcasts of society. Today this makes up a realm of transients, the chronically unemployed, beggars, alcoholics and drug derelicts, and others without any regular connection to the social order. Weber (1922/1968: 486) provides a historical analogy to their culture in his discussion of the religious propensities of slaves, a dispossessed group shunted around in the wars of ancient societies. He describes them as disinclined to have any religious beliefs and participation at all, which is parallel to the way today's lower class is more or less completely isolated, outside the main legitimating themes of modern culture. When such a group does get mobilized religiously, however, it takes a very violent emotion to do it, a wave of panic or hope when the social order is severely shaken. Historically this has been manifested in chiliastic movements, fantastic beliefs about the imminent destruction of the world or the imminent coming of divine intervention. Such emotional movements have had their modern secular counterpart, too. The urban lower class, usually immobilized politically, nevertheless has been thrown into the cauldron of political events during some of the great revolutions, as well as in the riots and insurrections of the past few centuries, and even in our own day.

WEBER'S CONTRIBUTION TO SOCIOLOGY

There is much more that could be developed from *Economy and Society*, and indeed from all of Weber's works. His analysis of bureaucracy provides the basis for the modern theory of organizations. When we see this in a properly sophisticated way, we find that it delineates all the major ingredients we need, not only the formal structure—the bureaucratic side—but also the informal structure, which Weber treated as the ideal type that goes along with it. There is always an informal structure of groups inside the organization, of loyalties to persons rather than to abstract rules and regulations, and Weber expresses this in such a way that the two ideal types— bureaucracy and patrimonialism—mesh together in various situations to make up the actual concrete organization. Weber's view of organizations is of various methods used for control, and a resulting struggle for power among the different factions of the organization. His theory of bureaucracy lays out some of the conditions in the realm of material resources, communications, and legitimation that create different sorts of organizational structures. The interested reader is referred to my *Conflict Sociology* (Collins, 1975: chap. 6) for elaboration.

Looking back over all the material we have covered in the chapters of this book, we see that Weber had a vision of world history. He never completed this part of his work; there were at least three more studies of the great world religions still to be written (Islam, early Christianity, medieval Christianity), and we cannot be entirely sure what he would have come up with, and possibly even where he might have changed his mind. An effort has been made to reconstruct his argument for Islam (Turner, 1974); and I have tried to extrapolate what he would have said about the European Middle Ages (in Collins, 1986, chap. 3). Here, I suggest, Weber would have had to revise his writings. For the full institutional model of capitalism that he developed, especially in his *General Economic History,* when applied to that period, yields the result that the real transformation occurred not during the Reformation, but in the High Middle Ages (ca. 1000-1300 A.D.) and in the institutions of the Catholic church rather than later, in the advent of Protestantism. (Hence I have called this the "Weberian Revolution of the High Middle Ages.") Applying the same argument of China (in Collins, 1986: chap. 3), I point out that Weber did not pay enough attention to Buddhism in the Chinese Middle Ages (ca. 400-900 A.D.), where a quasi-capitalist economic takeoff was also produced. These arguments, if true, do not invalidate Weber's general theory of world history, though they do modify its application to the actual unfolding of events. After all, it is Weber's theory that I am applying here. But that is the mark of a good theory: that it be progressive, that it contain implications that can be further worked out, and that it lead beyond itself.

By this criterion, Weber is a very great theorist indeed. We are very far from having made the fullest use of his theories, in order to develop our own sociology to the maximal extent. The process is still going on. Weber's works contain, for example, a theory of politics as a struggle for legitimacy, in which a state's position in the external world (its military and social prestige) is the key to the dynamic of political events. (I have tried to spell this out, as well as develop the theory further, in my *Weberian Sociological Theory,* Collins, 1986: chaps. 5-7.) Weber also has a theory of the family, based on comparative evidence, that puts political as well as economic factors back into the analysis of that institution. It gives a very illuminating perspective on the family across world history that meshes well with the lively current research on that topic; and it is of special interest for us now, because it deals directly with sexual stratification, with the positions of men and women, which is a major intellectual topic as well as social controversy of today. (This is elaborated in Collins, 1986: chaps. 11-12.) Here as elsewhere Weber continues to be very contemporary in his theoretical relevance.

There is a lot more to be done. At various points I have touched on some of Weber's contributions that have not yet been sufficiently worked into a more general theoretical form. In the discussion of rationalization, for example (Chapter 4), I examined Weber's sociology of music. In many ways, this is still at the forefront of our theoretical knowledge, because it has been rare for scholars to make the kinds of comparisons Weber did and to draw out a theoretical structure from them. It remains for a sociologist of our times to take over what Weber accomplished, and to go on from there to produce a genuinely comparatively based sociology of music. Weber's work on the *Agrarian Sociology of Ancient Civilizations*, similarly, is another untapped gold mine, waiting for a modern scholar to extract its theoretical relevance. Weber's discussion of ethnic groups, too, when seen in the light of his general theory of the creation of status groups, remains a leading candidate for establishing a real sociological theory in this area, which as yet remains rather undertheoretized. We have been too concerned with describing the details of what is happening to the ethnic (including racial) groups in our own society today to see that this can only be well understood with the kind of theory that comes from a comparative vision. Here again Weber has left us a legacy that has yet to be fully claimed.

There is a tendency now for us to adulate the thinkers of the past. We treat them as figures of a heroic age, and act as if there is nothing we can do of comparable worth. We put ourselves in the position of writing commentaries on the classics, writing their histories and putting them in the context of their times, not of our own. This is a legitimate form of scholarship. But to treat Weber in this way is to miss what is most important about his work. However fascinating his own times were, in some respects they are just like our own. He lived in a world in which scholars pursued specialties, and wrote the history of past ideas rather than trying to develop theories relevant in the present. Weber himself, in his methodological writings, tended to adulate the interpretation of history, and to downgrade theoretical generalizations. Nevertheless, we are fortunate that he was greater than his own methodology, and that he did provide a wealth of theory for our use. Our own stance ought to be to use Weber as an inspiration, the model of a kind of work we should try to carry on ourselves.

References

ALEXANDER, JEFFREY C. (1983) Theoretical Logic in Sociology, Vol. 3: The Classical Attempt at Theoretical Synthesis: Max Weber. Berkeley: University of California Press.

ANDERSON, PERRY (1974) Passages from Antiquity to Feudalism. London: New Left Books.

BENDIX, REINHARD and GUENTHER ROTH (1971) Scholarship and Partisanship: Essays on Max Weber. Berkeley: University of California Press.

COLLINS, RANDALL (1975) Conflict Sociology. New York: Academic Press.

——(1986) Weberian Sociological Theory. New York: Cambridge University Press.

GREEN, MARTIN (1974) The Von Richthofen Sisters. New York: Basic Books.

KALBERG, STEPHEN (1979) "The search for thematic orientations in a fragmented oeuvre: the discussion of Max Weber in recent German sociological literature." Sociology 13: 127-139.

——(1980) "Max Weber's types of rationality." American Journal of Sociology 85: 1145-1179.

MILLS, C. WRIGHT (1956) The Power Elite. New York: Oxford University Press.

MITZMAN, ARTHUR (1970) The Iron Cage. New York: Knopf.

MOMMSEN, WOLFGANG (1985) Max Weber and German Politics. 1890-1920 (1959). Chicago: University of Chicago Press.

PARSONS, TALCOTT (1937) The Structure of Social Action. New York: McGraw-Hill.

——(1947) "Introduction," in M. Weber, The Theory of Social and Economic Organization. (A. M. Henderson and T. Parsons, trans.). New York: Oxford University Press.

——(1963) "Introduction," in Max Weber, The Sociology of Religion (E. Fischoff, trans.). Boston: Beacon.

SAMUELSSON, KURT (1961) Religion and Economic Action. New York: Basic Books.

SCHLUCHTER, W. (1981) The Rise of Western Rationalism. Berkeley: University of California Press.

SCHUMPETER, JOSEPH A. (1954) History of Economic Analysis. New York: Oxford University Press.

STONE, LAWRENCE (1967) The Crisis of the Aristocracy, 1558-1641. New York: Oxford University Press.

TAWNEY, R. H. (1938) Religion and the Rise of Capitalism. Baltimore: Penguin.

TENBRUCK, F. H. (1975) "Das Werk Max Webers." Koelner Zeitschrift für Soziologie und Sozialpsychologie 27: 663-702.

TURNER, BRIAN S. (1974) Weber and Islam. London: Routledge & Kegan Paul.

WEBER, MARIANNE (1975) Max Weber: A Biography (1926). New York: John Wiley. (Translation of Max Weber: Ein Lebensbild)

WEBER, MAX (1930) The Protestant Ethic and the Spirit of Capitalism (T. Parsons, trans.) (1904-1905). New York: Scribner's.

———(1946) From Max Weber: Essays in Sociology (H. H. Gerth and C. W. Mills, eds. and trans.). New York: Oxford University Press.

———(1947) The Theory of Social and Economic Organization (A. M. Henderson and T. Parsons, trans.) (1922). New York: Oxford University Press.

———(1949) The Methodology of the Social Sciences (E. A. Shils and H. A. Finch, trans.) (1904, 1906, 1917-1919). New York: Free Press.

———(1951) The Religion of China (H. H. Gerth, trans.) (1916). New York: Free Press. (Originally published in Archiv für Sozialwissenschaft und Sozialforschung).

———(1952) Ancient Judaism. (H. H. Gerth and D. Martindale, trans.) (1917-1919). New York: Free Press. (Originally published in Archiv für Sozialwissenschaft und Sozialforschung)

———(1954) Max Weber on Law in Economy and Society (E. Shils and M. Rheinstein, trans.) (1922). Cambridge, MA: Harvard University Press.

———(1958a) The Rational and Social Foundations of Music (D. Martindale et al., trans.) (1911). Carbondale: Southern Illinois University Press.

———(1958b) The City (D. Martindale and G. Neuwirth, trans.) (1922). New York: Free Press.

———(1958c) The Religion of India (H. H. Gerth and D. Martindale, trans.) (1916-1917). New York: Free Press. (Originally published in Archiv für Sozialwissenschaft und Sozialforschung)

———(1961) General Economic History (F. H. Knight, trans.) (1923). New York: Collier-Macmillan. (Originally from 1919-1920 lectures)

———(1963) The Sociology of Religion (E. Fischoff, trans.) (1922). Boston: Beacon.

———(1968) Economy and Society (G. Roth and K. Wittich, eds.) (1922). New York: Bedminster.

———(1975) Roscher and Knies: The Logical Problems of Historical Economics (1903-1906). New York: Free Press. (Originally published in Schmoller's Jahrbuch)

———(1976) The Agrarian Sociology of Ancient Civilizations (1909) London: New Left Books.

WILEY, NORBERT F. (1967) "America's unique class politics: the interplay of the labor, credit, and commodity markets." American Sociological Review 32: 529-540.

———(1983) "On the congruence of Weber and Keynes," Randall Collins (ed.) Sociological Theory. San Francisco: Jossey-Bass.

Name Index

Alexander, Jeffrey, 11, 143
Anderson, Perry, 82, 143

Bohm-Bawerk, Eugen von, 40

Calvin, John, 49, 50

Dilthey, Wilhelm, 34, 35

Engels, Freidrich, 100

Fichte, Johann Gottleib, 33
Fischoff, Ephraim, 125, 144
Freud, Sigmund, 16, 22, 23, 26, 36

Gerth, Hans, 125, 144
Goethe, Johann Wolfgang von, 37
Gross, Otto, 22, 23

Haberman, Gustav, 11
Hegel, Georg Wilhelm Freidrich, 33, 37

Jaffe, Edgar, 21
Jellinek, Georg, 29
Jevons, William Stanley, 38

Kant, Immanuel, 33, 34

Lederer, Emil, 126
Luther, Martin, 48, 49, 56, 57

Martindale, Don, 125, 144
Marx, Karl, 31, 36, 37, 38, 51, 55, 56, 85, 100
Menger, Karl, 38, 39, 40
Mills, C. Wright, 10, 11, 125, 143, 144

Mommsen, Theodor, 28, 143

Naumann, Friedrich, 17
Nietzsche, Friedrich Wilhelm, 36

Parsons, Talcott, 45, 62, 125, 128, 143, 144

Rheinstein, Max, 125, 144
Ricardo, David, 38, 39
Rickert, Heinrich, 29, 34
Roth, Guenther, 126, 144

Samuelsson, K., 52, 143
Schelling, 33, 37
Schluchter, Wolfgang, 11, 62, 143
Schmoller, Gustav, 38, 39, 40, 41
Schopenhauer, Arthur, 36
Schumpeter, Joseph, 126, 143
Schutz, Alfred, 11
Shils, Edward, 125, 144
Smith, Adam, 38, 39, 87
Sombart, Werner, 87, 126
Stone, Laurence, 52, 143

Tawney, R. H., 52, 144
Tenbruck, Friedrich, 62, 144
Troeltsch, Ernst, 29

von Richthofen, Else, 20, 21

Walras, Leon, 38
Weber, Helene, 15-28 passim
Weber, Marianne, 11-29 passim, 33, 144
Weber, Max, Sr., 15-28 passim
Windelband, Wilhelm, 34, 35
Wittich, Claus, 126, 144

Subject Index

Action: emotional, 43, 44; rational, 45, traditional, 43, 44
Action theory, 42-45; means-rationality, 62; value-rationality, 62
Archiv für Sozialwissenschaft, 21, 26, 29, 32
Archive for Social Science. See *Archive für Sozialwissenschaft*
Asceticism, rationally active, 71

Battle of methods, See *Methodenstreit*
Buddhism. See China, religions of; India, religions of
Bureaucracy: as ideal type, 34, 138; as organization, 42, 62, 83, 138; as a menace, 68

Calling: doctrine of, 56; concept of, 94
Calvinists: and the elect, 50, 51; and predestination, 50, 51
Capital accounting, 83, 84, 86
Capitalism: ancient, 98-104; and the aristocracy, 52; and the bourgeoisie, 52; causal chain, 86-94; components of, 89, Fig. 1; definition of, 83; modern, 42, 43, 53; rational, 53, 62; and religion, 31, 47, 49, 55, 92-94; the rise of, 83-86; traditional, 53, 62
Catholicism: as obstacle to capitalism, 56-58
China: clan system, 119-120; ethics, 119; religions of, 105, 118-124; religious motivation in, 122
Citizenship, 90, 91
Civilizations, ancient, 97-99

Class: consciousness, 134; lower, 134; middle, 134; upper, 134-135; working, 134
Classes, 132; economic, 133; religious tendencies of, 135; social, 134; special, 133
Comparative sociology: historical, 130; as a systematic theory, 129-132; of whole societies, 130
Conflict: between idealism and realism, 17; theory, 97, 127; Weber's approach to, 45
Confucianism. See China, religions of
Counter-Reformation, 59

Distribution, 54

Economic development: and religious ideas, 52
Economics: Austrian/ English neoclassical school, 38-41; classical, 38; German historical school, 38-41; marginalist, 38
Economists: historical, 39; institutional, 39
Economy, market, 40
Encyclopedia of political science, 26
Epistemological idealism, 33, 37
Ethnomethodology, 11
Evangelical-Social Congress, 16, 24
Evolutionism, rationalist, 11

Family: Weber's theory of, 139
Feminism, 21, 22, 25, 28
Feminist movement, 25
Financial transactions, 87, 90

Geistewissenschaft, 35, 36
Geographical conditions, 91

German historical camp, 41
German Sociological Association, 26
German Sociological Society, 13

Hinduism. See India, religions of
Human sciences. See *Geistewissenschaft*

Idealism: aesthetic, 37, 38; dialectical, 37;
epistemological, 33-34, 37; historicist,
34-35; naturalist, 36-37
Ideal type: analysis, 47, 53; laissez-faire
economy as, 85
Ideal types, 32, 34; and action theory, 42; as
a comparative method, 131; doctrine
of, 29, 32, 41; method of, 40; and
rationality, 70; as a tool, 35; as a
weapon, 38, 41
Ideographic knowledge, 35
India: caste system, 112-118; reincarnation,
116-118; religions of, 105, 111-118; religious ethic of, 118
Industrial Revolution, 52; and modern
economy, 85
Investment of money, 55

Jainism. See India, religions of
Judaism, ancient, 105, 106-111; Christianity, a branch of, 111; and ethics, 108;
monotheistic, 108; prophets, 108, 109,
110; religious motivations, 110; taboos
and rituals, 110; Yahwe Confederacy,
107-108

Karma. See India, reincarnation

Labor: free, 84, 88; slave, 87
Laissez-faire, 40, 85
Legal system/law, 84, 87, 89, 91
Liberals, nineteenth century, 40

Marginalist revolution, 38, 39
Marginal utility theory, 38, 39, 40
Market: consumer, 86; mass, 54, 55 87;
neoclassical, 40
Market system: predictability of, 63; ration-
al, 63; regularity of, 63

Marxian theory, 85
Marxists, 41
Mass market, 54, 55, 87
Mass production, 54, 86, 88; for war, 87
Means-ends-rationality, 42, 43, 44
Means versus ends, doctrine of, 36
Mechanization, 86
Mental breakdown, Weber's, 12; before,
24; causes of, 14-22; conflict between
mother and father, 14; during, 32; per-
sonality, a key to, 27; recovery, 29, 32;
result of, 26; and sexual tension, 18-22;
symptoms of, 15; work before and
after, 13-14
Methodenstreit, 38-42
Methodological arguments, 41, 42
Methodological writings, 31, 32, 37, 38
Methodology, 32
Methods, the battle of. See *Methodenstreit*
Middle Ages, European, economy of, 103,
104
Military conditions, 92
Monasteries/monasticism, 48, 56-58, 73-
74, 75
Monks: as religious "virtuosi," 48
Munich, University of, 13, 25
Music: as rationalization, 63-69; sociology
of, 140
Mysticism, 71, 75, 76

Natural science. See *Naturwissenschaft*
Naturwissenschaft, 35
Neoclassical economic theory, 40
Neoclassical market economy, 41, 85
Nomothetic knowledge, 35

Organization, modern: theory of, 11
Organizations: models of, 131; sociology
of, 132

Pacifism: moral issue of, 27; Weber's opposition to, 25
Parsonian functionalism, 10, 11, 45
Patrimonialism: as an ideal type, 34, 138; in
organization, 138
Politics: sociology of, 132; as a struggle,
131, 139; theory of, 10

About the Author

Randall Collins is Professor of Sociology at the University of California, Riverside. He has taught at the Universities of California at Berkeley, Los Angeles, and San Diego, and the Universities of Wisconsin, Virginia, and Chicago. Among his books are *Conflict Sociology* (1975), *The Credential Society* (1979), *Sociology Since Midcentury* (1981), *Three Sociological Traditions* (1985), and *Weberian Sociological Theory* (1986).

WOLVERHAMPTON
POLYTECHNIC LIBRARY

NOTES

311
D/3

WOLVERHAMPTON
POLYTECHNIC LIBRARY